1.50

M.

MAY 2 4 1988

Le Cid

A Translation in Rhymed Couplets

PIERRE CORNEILLE

Le Cid

A Translation in Rhymed Couplets

by

Vincent J. Cheng

DELAWARE

Newark: University of Delaware Press
London and Toronto: Associated University Presses

Associated University Presses
440 Forsgate Drive
Cranbury, NJ 08512

Associated University Presses
25 Sicilian Avenue
London WC1A 2QH, England

Associated University Presses
2133 Royal Windsor Drive
Unit 1
Mississauga, Ontario
Canada L5J 1K5

The paper used in this publication meets the requirements
of the American National Standard for Permanence of Paper
for Printed Library Materials Z39.48-1984.

Library of Congress Cataloging-in-Publication Data

Corneille, Pierre, 1606–1684.
    Le Cid : a translation in rhymed couplets.

    Translation of: Le Cid.
    Bibliography: p.
    1. Cid, ca. 1043–1099—Drama.   I. Title.
PQ1749.E5C44   1987   842'.4   85-40877
ISBN 0-87413-294-0 (alk. paper)

Printed in the United States of America

To the memory of my father,

Johnson Cheng

Contents

Preface

My earliest childhood recollection of a literary sort may have been the time my father (a career diplomat and a former French major in college in China) met an old college friend (and fellow French major) whom he had not seen in many years, at the airport in Mexico City (or was it in Brazil?), where we were then stationed. To my surprise, they did not greet each other in Chinese; rather, the friend accosted my father with machine-gun sharpness: "Rodrigue, as-tu du coeur?"—to which my father replied, without hesitation: "Tout autre que mon père / L'éprouverait sur l'heure!" (*Le Cid*, lines 261–62). And the two of them then laughed with pleasure at still remembering this famed and favorite exchange from their student years. Nothing about the incident struck my child's sensitivity then as being odd (certainly not the likelihood of two Chinese diplomats meeting at a Mexican airport and spouting seventeenth-century French couplets), except this: I was amazed that a book or play or poem (and *Le Cid* is all three) could affect people enough to become part of a friendship—and that I must someday read this play so dear to my own father. (Ironic legacy, since *Le Cid* is a play largely about filial obligation.) Eventually, I found among my parents' record albums an old disc of La Comédie Française performing *Le Cid* with Gérard Philipe in the title role. I would listen to that strange and incomprehensible record from time to time—like a kitten listening to the song of a cicada—and grew to understand bits of it as I learned more and more French in school. That was the germination of my interest in literature.

Much later, when I myself was a college student (and English major: my older sister had already become a French major, and I decided that two in the family were enough) at Harvard, I had the good fortune one year of studying English versification with Robert Fitzgerald, the wonderful classical translator and poet, at the same time that I was treating myself to a course on the *théâtre classique* with the great French scholar Paul Bénichou. These two

9

interests merged into a serendipitous idea, and, under Mr. Fitzgerald's guidance, I began a labor of love (and, I discovered, of great pleasure): an English couplet translation of *Le Cid*.

Despite Mr. Fitzgerald's encouragement that I should publish my translation, other personal and professional distractions (including the death of my father) soon intervened; that original draft lay untouched in a box in a closet for many years. A couple of years ago, I brought it out of mothballs and showed it to some colleagues of mine at the University of Southern California. They liked it and suggested I publish it; to my surprise, I found that I, too, still liked much of what I had written. I rewrote or revised the rest, again reacquainting myself with the pure pleasure of the endeavor.

In the process of revising the translation, I carefully looked into existing verse translation theory and methodology. I also surveyed previous English verse translations of *Le Cid*, only one of which—unfortunately the worst, in my view—had attempted rhymed couplets, a demanding form which nevertheless seems to me essential to the spirit and qualities of French classical drama. And Richard Wilbur's couplet translations of Molière and Racine have shown that there is an educated audience receptive to good couplet translations of French classical drama. Subsequently, I prepared an essay discussing the problems and advantages of rhymed translation, comparing passages from various previous translations of *Le Cid;* this essay has become the Introduction to my translation. Finally, I prepared the extensive "Backgrounds and Discussion" chapters to provide the reader with relevant and helpful information and critical perspectives on Corneille's *Le Cid*, one of the great master works of the French literary canon.

This verse translation would have been neither written nor published without the guidance and encouragement of a number of people to whom I am much indebted. At Harvard, the original draft benefited from the perceptive scrutiny of Monroe Engel, William Alfred, and R. H. Chapman. At Boston University, George Starbuck and John Malcolm Brinnin made some helpful suggestions; so did Ned Spofford at Stanford University. More recently, my colleagues in Los Angeles have also been generous with their advice and encouragement—especially Virginia Tufte and Allan Casson at the University of Southern California, Richard Yarborough at the University of California at Los Angeles, and Wendy Furman at Whittier College. Some welcome information on the earliest English translations of *Le Cid* was provided by S. Y. Huang, the family "friend" mentioned in the first paragraph above. The final draft owes much to the insightful reading and excellent suggestions by Theodore E. D. Braun of the University of Delaware's French department. And I am grateful to the editors at the University of Delaware Press, especially to the judicious ear of Donald C. Yelton.

Finally, however, two persons were most essentially responsible for the genesis and writing of this work: my father and Robert Fitzgerald. They were Odysseus and Mentor to this Telemachus. I wish they were both alive to read this.

Introduction

An Argument for Rhymed Translation of Rhymed Drama

Rudyard Kipling commented on the composing of poetry thus:

> There are nine and sixty ways of constructing tribal lays
> And every single one of them is right!
>
> ("In the Neolithic Age")

One might be tempted to extend this logic to verse translation: there are many possible ways of translating foreign lays—and every single one of *them* is right? Every one of them, certainly, may be a poem in itself. But with translation, I would suggest, some ways are perhaps more right than others; since translations attempt to achieve a close equation (or at least an equivalence) to the original lay, one might say (to paraphrase Orwell) that some ways are more equal than others.

My intention here is certainly not to make an argument for the validity of verse translations. Our century has already made the point eloquently, both through actual translations and by scholarly argument. Poet-translators such as Ezra Pound, C. Day Lewis, Vladimir Nabokov, Robert Lowell, W. S. Merwin, Dudley Fitts, Robert Fitzgerald, and Richard Wilbur—have begun to restore English verse translation to the stature it once enjoyed, when Chapman and later Pope wrote their translations of Homer. More recently, the analysis and methodology of poetic translation has become an accepted discipline for literary study:[1] there has been a spate of serious studies, from the Harvard Studies volume *On Translation* to George Steiner's *After Babel*, from Nabokov's notes on translating Pushkin to André Lefevere's systematic analysis of available methodologies; lately John Felstiner has come out with his volume on translating Neruda, in which Professor Felstiner ultimately argues that translation is itself an act of literary criticism. In short, verse translation has reestablished itself as a legitimate art form, as well as a valid topic for critical study and analysis.[2]

My intention in this essay, rather, is to argue a very particular point: the importance of translating rhymed verse drama into rhymed English verse—as opposed to the usual practice by English verse-drama translators of resorting to blank verse. And I shall do so through a discussion about translating Pierre Corneille's masterwork of the French *théâtre classique, Le Cid*.

Why *Le Cid?* To begin with, French drama in general and its classical period in particular are good sources for such a study, since they provide a preponderance of plays written completely in rhymed verse. In this sense, the French drama of the 1600s was totally unlike its Elizabethan and Jacobean counterparts in England, where rhyme was used occasionally in serious drama, but never exclusively or even to any major extent. The concept of the rhymed couplet was not simply crucial to, but a defining essence of French classical drama. Granted the accessibility, then, of French classical theatre for such a study of translating rhymed drama, the choice of *Le Cid* is an especially convenient one for discussion: it is a standard school text for French students, and thus is perhaps, along with Molière's *Tartuffe* or Racine's *Phèdre,* the best known work of *le grand siècle*—the French seventeenth century, as well known to French students as *Macbeth* or *Julius Caesar* to English ones.

Furthermore, translations of Corneille into English face a particularly stiff and revealing test to begin with: while Molière's comic satire and Racine's psychological insights appeal to the contemporary sensibility, few modern-day English speakers really understand or appreciate Corneille's strength—his stylized, heroic, and neo-bombastic rhetoric. And if a translation does not even try to provide a sense of this stylization, its English reader is inevitably at a loss to comprehend, even minimally, why *Le Cid* was ever such a celebrated achievement.

And finally, *Le Cid* is a good choice for study because, as a masterwork of French literature, it has been translated a number of times into English verse—eight different previously published versions, as far as I can ascertain, in this century. Of these eight, all but one have been largely in blank verse.[3] Although all the blank verse translations have their own commendable qualities, the sole couplet translation is the one clear failure of the lot—a stiff, unnatural victim of its own inability to rhyme and speak English at the same time. Thus, it provides more fuel for Professor Lefevere's contention that "the rhyming translator fights a losing battle against the limitations he imposes on himself . . . and . . . is doomed to failure from the start."[4]

What should be the aims in a verse-drama translation? Well, the three words define themselves. First and foremost, it should be *verse*, should be able to stand on its own five feet as verse of good quality. Secondly, it should be able to function as *drama:* it should be natural, speakable, and believable as staged dialogue. Finally, it is a *translation,* and thus should translate faithfully. In a verse translation, there are two aspects to "faithfulness": there is not purely that of accuracy in rendering precise meanings, ideas, and tones, but also the accuracy of rendering, or imitating, the verse and verse forms of the original—in other words, not just *what* is said in the original, but *how* it is said, for the beauty, form, and style of the expression are, after all, what distinguish a faithful verse translation from a faithful prose translation.[5]

We should get no argument here: no one would dispute that form and meaning are inseparable—and that in form there is meaning, that the versification and style of a poem, to some degree, reflect the thought processes, logic, principles, and conventions that produced it: the author, the milieu, and the age that spawned the work.[6] This is a particularly important point when dealing with the culture and period that produced *le théâtre classique,* with its peculiar, rigorous conventions and values, so alien to modern American society. The harsh controls and self-imposed rigors in its poetry reflect a society with similarly strict and arbitrary moral and social codes of behavior. (Corneille himself, in his obsession with honor, duty, true love, reputation, and so forth, was more faithful to the concerns of France in his own age than to those of medieval Spain, where the story takes place.) The notions of the attainment of freedom within the confines of a discipline, of beauty in surmounting the difficulties—these are reflections of seventeenth-century France, particularly of its genteel classes, as well as the underlying principles in its dramatic verse. The orderly precision and balance of the lines, and of the ideas and logic within those lines, mirror an optimism and belief in an ordered universe not unlike that found in Pope's verse nearly a century later, in England.

So no one would dispute that, in the best of all possible worlds, a translation must imitate form to achieve proper meaning—and, in such an ideal world, an English translation of *Le Cid* should, no doubt, be written in alexandrine couplets, broken every six syllables by a hemistichal *césure,* and all in alternating masculine and feminine rhymes! But such an impossibility is attainable only in the world of Borges's Pierre Menard.

But it *is* important that a verse translation produce as close a feeling for the original verse as possible within the poetic bounds of the language of translation. Although there have been several blank verse translations of *Le Cid,* these are by nature not "faithful" renditions in the sense of that word as discussed earlier.

So there we have the basic problem. Versificatory reproduction is desirable but difficult and perhaps impossible. What is one to do? Let us approach the problem first by looking at the difficulties of writing a couplet translation—ideally, of course, the more "faithful" form.

The first and most obvious difficulty is that a play is a *long* work: it is one thing to translate a twenty-line poem by Gautier or Rimbaud into twenty lines of rhymed English verse; it is another thing altogether to contemplate the Sisyphean labor of finding rhymes for two thousand lines of dramatic verse,[7] which have also to be translated.

Secondly, the Latinate facility in rhyming does not exist in English, making the masculine-feminine rhyme scheme quite inconceivable (unless by excessive distortions of meaning and syntax) on an extended scale. Rather, we are forced to be content to achieve rhyming couplets at all, regardless of their sexual persuasion.

Furthermore, the alexandrine (twelve-syllable) line has been repeatedly proven to be foreign and unsuitable to English. And so, in order to follow a meter more natural to English (and the most accepted one in its poetic drama), the logical choice is iambic pentameter, a meter whose rhythms and conventions have proven marvelously adaptable to the English language. Thus, our natural choice, by force of necessity, for a rhymed translation of *Le Cid*, is the iambic pentameter, or "heroic," couplet (appropriate since we are dealing with "heroic" drama).[8]

But still we are besieged by difficulties. It is hard enough to write rhymed verse to begin with, but to do so in translation is doubly hard: one has to find not only appropriate rhymes, but rhymes that fit the meaning prescribed by the equivalent lines of the original. Let me illustrate. James Schevill, in his couplet translation of *Le Cid*, repeatedly falls victim to the demands of rhyme at the expense of sense. The first example is only a slight distortion of *mes yeux ont vu son sang* (line 659: act 2, scene 8—literally, "my eyes have seen his blood")—

> CHIMENE: *Sire, mon père est mort; mes yeux ont vu son sang*
> *Couler à gros bouillons de son généreux flanc.*

Mr. Schevill translates:

> My father, Sire, is dead. No one can hide
> The stream of blood that gushed from his torn side.

Mr. Schevill clearly needed a rhyme for "side," and came up with "No one can hide." The reader may swallow this distortion because Corneille's general idea is maintained (though "torn" does not render *généreux*).[9] More troublesome and more frequent, unfortunately, is the sort of compromise exemplifed six lines later:

> CHIMENE: *J'ai couru sur le lieu, sans force et sans couleur;*
> *Je l'ai trouvé sans vie. Excusez ma douleur. . . .*

Mr. Schevill:

> Trembling and pale I ran to that grim place;
> I found him dead. Avenge, Sire, this disgrace.

The necessity of a rhyme for "place" leads to an inexcusable substitution of "Avenge, Sire, this disgrace" for *Excusez ma douleur* ("Pardon my grief"). Finally, Mr. Schevill is at times such a slave to rhyme that he even resorts to couplets of the sort below:

> RODRIGUE: *Je me suis accusé de trop de violence;*
> *Et ta beauté sans doute emportait la balance.*
>
> (885–86: 3.4)

Mr. Schevill's version is incomprehensible (but it does, alas, rhyme):

> My choice was cold disgrace or loss of love,
> I thought of you as gentle as a dove.

Rhyming "love" with "gentle as a dove" is a cliché at which even early rock-and-roll lyricists would have been embarrassed.

In any case, rhyming nearly two thousand lines, when one's word choices are severely limited by the prescriptions and proscriptions of the lines translated, is clearly not a task easily undertaken for love or dove.

Nor does our choice of metrical form relieve the difficulties. To begin with, in writing iambic pentameter, one adopts the "rules," conventions, and traditions of that meter in English. The French alexandrine depends simply on a syllabic count, since French is a comparatively nonaccentual language. However, English pentameter has an accentual-syllabic tradition, so that, in addition to the strictures of a syllabic count, the poet must also observe an iambic pattern within conventionally accepted limits of substitution; he must count both syllables *and* accents. Thus, for example, faced with the first line of Don Diègue's famed soliloquy in 1.4 (line 237)—

> *O rage! ô désespoir! ô vieillesse ennemie!*

—we are tempted to translate thus:

> O rage! O despair! O hateful old age!

This translation has the required ten syllables, is semantically and rhetorically faithful, and fashions a thematically appropriate and aesthetically appealing internal rhyme (rage/age). But it does not scan, no matter how one tries, as iambic pentameter:

ᵕ ˊ ᵕ ᵕ ˊ ᵕ ˊ ᵕ ᵕ ˊ
O rage! O despair! O hateful old age!

Rather, we must make some concessions and adjustments. Lacy Lockert, for example, changes "rage" to "fury" to make the line scan:

O fury! O despair! Hateful old age!

I have chosen to keep the diction, but to change the speaking voice from vocative to imperative:

Rage and despair at old, despisèd age!

Both of these versions maintain our accentual-syllabic pattern of five iambic feet (including an acceptable trochaic substitution).[10]

As if the constraints of syllabic as well as accentual counts were not enough to add onto the demands of rhyme,[11] there is the difficulty that, in translating from alexandrines to pentameter, one loses two syllables per line. Thus, not only does the English translator face greater difficulties in rhyming as well as in meter, he must do his job in four fewer syllables per couplet. Attempting to render the French faithfully in style and sense, line by line, as well as manipulating the diction and syntax so as to produce end-rhymes, all while suffering a two-syllable handicap per line—that's a challenge whose difficulty the classicists would have appreciated!

The two-syllable handicap, along with the rigors of rhyme and meter, have occasionally forced translators, all of whom profess to translate line-for-line (that is, each speech, passage, or remark should contain the same number of lines, or even of half-lines, as in the original) into a breakdown, into inserting unseemly extra lines or half-lines to complete the thought, or into changing the configuration of lines spoken by each speaker. Thus, this exchange between the Infante and Léonor in 83–85 (1.2)—

> INFANTE: *Je l'aime.*
> LEONOR: *Vous l'aimez!*
> INFANTE: *Mets la main sur mon coeur,*
> *Et vois comme il se trouble au nom de son vainqueur,*
> *Comme il le reconnaît.*
> LEONOR: *Pardonnez-moi, Madame . . .*

—rendered in three lines by Corneille, can only be squared by Mr. Schevill into four:

> INFANTE: Is still my love.
> LEONOR: For love you still pray?
> INFANTE: If you placed your soft hand upon my heart,
> It would confess by its impulsive start

How much I love him.

LEONOR: Madam, please excuse me . . .[12]

Still other difficulties lurk in readiness to ambush the unsuspecting rhymer. In addition to the self-imposed restrictions of form, we also have the delicate problem of style, in terms of tone and elevation. Any heroic drama rendered into modern English (in our nonheroic age) has a special handicap in that English couplets (unlike, say, Russian couplets) have had a "mock-heroic," quasi-comic tradition since the days of Pope and Swift: the same resounding rhymes present in intensely serious and elaborate French couplets or repartees often seem funny, silly, foppish, or excessively contrived when rendered into English.[13] Thus, it is easier to translate a comedy into English couplets, since the comic tradition is already present in English couplets—which may partly explain the success that Richard Wilbur's fine couplet translations of Molière have found on the American stage. *Le Cid*, alas, is a tragedy—or rather, a Cornelian *tragi-comédie*.

To nullify the "comic" handicap, we therefore must try somehow to follow the strict prosodic rules without allowing the versification, particularly the rhyme, to call undue attention to itself and thus run the risk of seeming to be silly contrivance; and yet, we also want the effects of resounding repartee, of concluding couplet, or of thumping rhetoric when they are called for. Thus, the rhyming translator must walk a stylistic tightrope while juggling various prosodic techniques: the modulations of pauses within the line, of enjambments, of "scudded" and inverted feet, and of stress variations—all techniques which help mute the potential jingle of the mock-heroic monotony.

And, lastly, there is the related problem of style of language. The contrived and inflated rhetoric of heroic conflicts and sentiments calls for a loftiness of tone problematic in modern English.[14] Deliberately lofty, poetic, archaic, or neo-Shakespearean language (with "thou, thine, methinks, it seemeth," and so forth) sounds silly and antiquated in a modern and spoken context—recall, after all, that this is *staged* drama. Florence Kendrick Cooper's 1904 translation of *Le Cid* illustrates this unsatisfactory solution to the problem of heroic tone. For example, her rendition of lines 440–42 (2.2):

COUNT: Art tired of life?
RODERICK: Dost thou, then, fear to die?
COUNT: Come on! Thou'rt right. I'll help theé do thy duty!
           'Tis a base son survives a father's fame.

Such lines read like a Hasty Pudding lampoon of Shakespeare, and, today, would be laughed right off the tragic stage.

Aware of this Charybdis, some translators have tried to steer hard by the Scylla of clear colloquialism and plain words. And yet, thoroughly colloquial expression and conversational idiom seem a total negation of the contrived, courtly quality of lofty, heroic classical tragedy. For example, Robert Lowell's couplet translation of Racine's *Phèdre* begins thus:

> HIPPOLYTUS: No, no, my friend, we're off! Six months have passed
> since Father heard the ocean howl and cast
> his galley on the Aegean's skull-white froth.
> Listen! The blank sea calls us—off, off, off!
> I'll follow Father to the fountainhead
> and marsh of hell. We're off. Alive or dead,
> I'll find him.

The passage certainly has dramatic vitality and plausible modern idiom. But this breathless hero ("off, off, off!") is not Hippolytus but Hotspur, or perhaps an Actors' Workshop aspirant strung out on caffein; he is too colloquial to capture the lofty majesty and controlled logic of Racine's opening couplets:

> *Le dessein en est pris: je pars, cher Théramène,*
> *Et quitte le séjour de l'aimable Trézène.*
> *Dans le doute mortel dont je suis agité,*
> *Je commence à rougir de mon oisiveté.*
> *Depuis plus de six mois éloigné de mon père,*
> *J'ignore le destin d'une tête si chère;*
> *J'ignore jusqu'aux lieux qui le peuvent cacher.*

It is inconceivable that the speaker of the celebrated and mellifluous "perfect" alexandrine, *La fille de Minos et de Pasiphaé* (line 36), could ever say, "Off, off, off!"[15]

Rather, we must steer a precarious middle course between Scylla and Charybdis. Thus, in our own age, where the "low style" seems to be the norm, in order to achieve the "high style," perhaps it is best to aim for what one might call the "middle style." In my own efforts, I have tried to attain a "middle style" that both captures the elevation of heroic sentiments and conserves the natural flexibility of the spoken language.

No paucity of challenges, then, for the rhyming translator: 1,840 lines of rhymed couplets, in ten-syllable iambic lines, maintaining the sense, tone, and lofty style of the original. Given all these difficulties, one may well ask, who would want even to try? Better to heed Professor Lefevere's warnings about rhyme; better, perhaps, to stick to blank verse, as most translators have done. Let Mr. Schevill—who, to give him his due, did at least dare take on the challenge—let Mr. Schevill's fate stand as a fair warning!

If rhymed translation, then, presents such extraordinary strictures, would it not be easier to detour the difficulties by translating into blank verse? Why rhyme at all?

Why indeed? Because, I would argue, the magnificent level of difficulty is in a sense the whole, and very, point. We come back to the issue of form and meaning; the rigors of the rhymed couplet are, in essence, a metaphor for the very quality of French classical verse: the imposition of order over chaos. Blank verse cannot mirror the same sense of imposed control and logic, a control which itself mirrors the very society which produced it. And, in that sense, form *is* meaning; the writing of rhymed couplets presents a challenge worthy of the classical strictures.

Corneille's action takes place in a world with a rigid, orderly, and known code of values, a ladder of priorities accepted by the courtly society of the play. And the verse form reflects this rigidity. In act 1, scene 6, Rodrigue undergoes a soul-searching soliloquy: what to do, faced with the conflicting demands of honor and love? He must either kill Chimène's father, vindicate his family name, and thus become her enemy; or else yield to his love for her and ignore his duty and reputation. In elaborately rhymed stanzas, Rodrigue inspects each alternative (including suicide) and its effects. The truly interesting epiphany in the monologue is Rodrigue's gradual realization that, really, he has *no choice* in the matter; the rhymed verses unerringly order his thought patterns, just as the social system of priorities undeviably directs him toward the one possible conclusion: he must kill Chimène's father. Rodrigue eventually reasons that, given a code of values in which honor ranks highest of all and which is accepted by everyone involved, were he *not* to kill Chimène's father, he would still lose her love anyway: after all, in such a case, she could no longer respect him, since, accepting the same code of values, she *expects* him as a man of honor to kill her father; not doing so, he is proved dishonorable and not worthy to be loved by her. The pure beauty of the code (and of the scene) lies in the formula: one need only apply the formula and code to a given situation, and out comes a single answer, based on the highest applicable priority in the value system. It is a rigidity of order imposed on the chaos of moral choice and relativism (and thus seems to me almost a nostalgic daydream of wish-fulfillment for our own relativistic century); the controlled rigidity of the logic is mirrored by the control and ordered patterns of the verse. Like Rodrigue in his soliloquy, the rhymed translator must struggle, and complain that "I'm bound by just yet difficult constraints" (line 312)—but realizes that his one honorable alternative is to try nevertheless to vanquish the difficulties, to play the game faithfully by the rules (to play tennis with a net, Frost might say). And first among these rules is the formulaic and rigid precision of the rhymed couplet, so essential a reflection of Corneille's world.

I had the good fortune, as a student, to study *le théâtre classique* with a great scholar of French classicism, Paul Bénichou, author of *Morales du Grand Siècle*.[16] My lecture notes from that period abound with Professor Bénichou's descriptions of the French classical tragedy, *le grand genre littéraire par excellence en France: la tragédie réglée, les règles d'austerité, un genre d'interdiction, une soumission des auteurs, le niveau de règles, l'idée de la difficulté vaincue* ("the great literary genre above all in France: the regulated tragedy, the rules of austerity, a genre of interdictions, a self-surrender by the authors, the level of regulations, the notion of overcoming difficulties"). All of these phrases reflect the classical formula of beauty as the surmounting of difficulties.

French classical tragedy was a literary genre imitating the tragedies of antiquity, and yoked to an interpretation (or misinterpretation) of Aristotle's dramatic unities. As such, all its authors submitted to this initial set of limitations: noble characters, noble and tragic subject matter, high and tragic tone, the unities of time, place, action; the genre was, by definition, one dominated by rules of austerity.

In addition to the classical interdictions, the genre was a "courtly" one, in the strict sense of that word—intended not for a popular audience, but for *la cour, les gens cultivés* (the court, the cultured class). The genre flourished because, in Professor Bénichou's words, *L'esthétique du théâtre classique est liée avec la vie à la cour* ("The aesthetics of the classical theatre are tied to the life at court"). The court itself was a central concentration of noblemen and ministers surrounding the king at Versailles; the monarchy exerted power by regulating the behavior in this group. And the society itself was regulated by a strict and demanding code of courtly and heroic values. Life at court was thus fraught at all times with tight interdictions and unlooked-for dangers. In this way, *Le Cid*'s concern with honor, duty, reputation, authority, and obligation is more reflective of the concerns of seventeenth-century Versailles than of eleventh-century Spain. One's own impulses and desires were, as in the play itself, constantly subject to regulation by *la gloire* (honor, glory) and by one's *devoir* (duty). And so, much of the aesthetic enjoyment of the genre by its cultured audience was as a metaphor for life: maintaining, but not crumbling under, *le niveau de règles* (the level of regulations)—grace under pressure, *les difficultés vaincues* (the difficulties surmounted).[17]

As Paul Landis writes in the "Introduction" to his *Le Cid*, "Here is a world in which personal honor is not a chemical reaction of gland secretions, but a self-instituted, self-administered rule of life. Here is a world which believes that man is master of himself and responsible for good and evil in his own conduct; a world in which nothing—not even life and love—is so precious as one's honor as a man. It is an old-fashioned, classical world, to be sure. . . ."[18] This is an ordered and regulated world mirrored by its main literary vehicle, with different emphases from the English poetic tradition. As Lacy Lockert writes in his own "Translator's Foreword": "Whereas we look in poetry for 'fine surprises' of language, play of imagination, depth and subtlety of thought, and detailed treatment of nature, a French classicist looks for orderly arrangement of ideas and for precision, lucidity, and euphony of expression."[19] Nowhere is this mania for order more evident and characteristic than in the discipline of the rhymed couplet.

The couplet is a form suited to the French Classical interdiction that no action and nothing mundane (no fight-sequences, murders, props, or Othellan handkerchiefs) may be seen on stage. Robbed of the crutch of physical *action* in a dramatic (or melodramatic) sense, the play must be carried by its own *rhetorical* action. To avoid being crushingly dull, the monologues and dialogues must be able effectively to replace staged sword-play with piercing repartee, sallies of stichomythia, and flourishes of finality when a point is driven home. The very logic and rhetoric of Corneille's characters depend on the couplet: theme, countertheme; witty reversal, or proverbial maxim. And always the tone must be controlled and elevated, with a quality of compact, well-turned perfection. For all of these purposes, the rhymed couplet is best suited.

Let us illustrate by comparing couplet and blank verse treatments of these rhetorical functions.

First of all, it is obvious that repartee occurs frequently in Corneille; the Count's argument with Don Diègue, for example, is a series of repartees:

> LE COMTE: *Ce que je méritais, vous l'avez emporté.*
> DON DIEGUE: *Qui l'a gagné sur vous l'avait mieux mérité.*
> LE COMTE: *Qui peut mieux l'exercer en est bien le plus digne.*
> DON DIEGUE: *En être refusé n'en est pas un bon signe.*
> LE COMTE: *Vous l'avez eu par brigue, étant vieux courtisan.*
> DON DIEGUE: *L'éclat de mes hauts faits fut mon seul partisan.*
> LE COMTE: *Parlons-en mieux, le Roi fait honneur à votre âge.*
> DON DIEGUE: *Le Roi, quand il en fait, le mesure au courage.*
> LE COMTE: *Et par là cet honneur n'était dû qu'à mon bras.*
> DON DIEGUE: *Qui n'a pu l'obtenir ne le méritait pas.*
>
> (215–24)

The importance of the answering rhyme (as a *touché!*, as in that last *pas*) is obvious, and doesn't require further elaboration or illustration.

Closely related, however, is Corneille's use of stichomythia (of which the above passage is also an example), often broken into hemistichal exchanges. The highly artificial, ceremonial technique of stichomythia reflects the styl-ized rhetoric and form of the genre. Let us first look at a lovely example in 984–88 (3.4):

> CHIMENE: *Mon unique souhait est de ne rien pouvoir.*
> RODRIGUE: *O miracle d'amour!*

> CHIMENE: *O comble de misères!*
> RODRIGUE: *Que de maux et de pleurs nous coûteront nos pères!*
> CHIMENE: *Rodrigue, qui l'eût cru?*
> RODRIGUE: *Chimène, qui l'eût dit?*
> CHIMENE: *Que notre heur fût si proche et sitôt se perdit?*

The lyrical power of these lines is undeniable. Chimène's admission that she can but hope to fail in her quest for vengeance is, for Rodrigue sweet music in his ears, but for Chimène a source of guilt and misery; their contrasting reactions are dramatically juxtaposed in a single, shared line: *O miracle d'amour! / O comble de misères!*—and the couplet then concludes with the key rhyme word *pères*—fathers, the source, after all, of this *comble de misères* (heap of miseries). The famous couplet which follows perfectly illustrates the rhetorical power of such an exchange—that sense of two speakers in a magical collaboration, completing the thought and couplet in joint composition of a lyrical rhyme:

> CHIMENE: *Rodrigue, qui l'eût cru?*
> RODRIGUE: *Chimène, qui l'eût dit?*
> CHIMENE: *Que notre heur fût si proche et sitôt se perdit?*

Clearly, neither of the above two couplets could achieve its effects without the rhyme. Of the blank verse translations of these four lines, the best in my opinion is Lacy Lockert's[20]—

> RODRIGUE: O miracle of love!
> CHIMENE: O weight of woe!
> RODRIGUE: What tears and misery our fathers cost us!
> CHIMENE: Roderick, who would have thought . . .
> RODRIGUE: Could have foretold . . .
> CHIMENE: That bliss so near us would so soon be lost!

Professor Lockert's lines are smooth and lyrical, but the reader experiences a letdown at the end of each couplet, where the clinching rhyme should be. My own version tries to maintain the lyrical qualities but also add the final touch of a jointly fashioned rhyme:

> RODRIGUE: O miracle of love!
> CHIMENE: O heavy pain!
> RODRIGUE: What woes our fathers force on us, Chimene!
> CHIMENE: Rodrigue, who would have known—
> RODRIGUE: —or thought to say—
> CHIMENE: That joy so near could so soon fly away?

There are many times when a speech should end with an assertive "oomph"—if such punch is needed, only a rhyme will do. For example,

Rodrigue concludes his bold challenge to the Count, who is undefeated in personal combat, thus:

> *J'attaque en téméraire un bras toujours vainqueur;*
> *Mais j'aurai trop de force, ayant assez de coeur.*
> *A qui venge son père il n'est rien impossible.*
> *Ton bras est invaincu, mais non pas invincible.*
>
> (415–18: 2.2)

As is often the case, Professor Lockert's blank verse is quite faithful:

> Yet I dare face an arm always victorious.
> He who is brave enough, hath might enough.
> One can do marvels in a father's cause.
> Thou art unconquered, not invincible.

The lines are crisp and commendable, but lack that end-speech flourish. I attempt them thus:

> But still I dare challenge your martial art.
> I'll find enough strength, having enough heart.
> For vengeance' sake, nothing's impossible;
> You're undefeated, not invincible.

Frequently, a similarly rhetorical and conclusive flourish occurs at the end of a scene. The play's very first scene ends with this exchange between Elvire and Chimène:

> ELVIRE: *Vous verrez cette crainte heureusement deçue.*
> CHIMENE: *Allons, quoi qu'il en soit, en attendre l'issue.*
>
> (57–58)

John Cairncross renders it passably, but sans flourish:

> ELVIRE: You'll see this fear most happily belied.
> CHIMENE: Let's wait the outcome, whatsoe'er it be!

I translate:

> ELVIRE: Your fears will vanish on this very day.
> CHIMENE: Well, we shall wait and see, let come what may.

Act 3, scene 4 ends with Chimène's troubled

> *Ne m'importune plus, laisse-moi soupirer,*
> *Je cherche le silence et la nuit pour pleurer.*
>
> (999—1000)

Florence Kendrick Cooper renders this couplet:

> Trouble me not; pray, leave me with my grief.
> I long for night's dark silence, and for tears.

My version:

> No more, Elvire—please leave me to my moan;
> I seek silence and night to weep alone.

A final example of this sort, in which unrhymed versions seem peculiarly awkward and inconclusive: act 4 ends with the King's command to Chimène—

> *Cesse de murmurer contre un arrêt si doux:*
> *Qui que ce soit des deux, j'en ferai ton époux.*
>
> (1463–64)

Paul Landis renders the couplet in blank verse:

> Cease your complaints against my mild decree:
> The victor of these two shall be your husband.

My own rhymed version attempts a click of crisp finality:

> Stop murmuring against such a sweet decree:
> You'll marry him who earns the victory.

Rhyme, of course, is also a mnemonic device; and Corneille employs its mnemonic qualities for dramatic effect, frequently echoing earlier lines in the play. For example, in lines 871–72, Rodrigue says to Chimène:

> *Car enfin n'attends pas de mon affection*
> *Un lâche repentir d'une bonne action.*

In the middle of her answering speech, Chimène responds with:

> *Car enfin n'attends pas de mon affection*
> *De lâches sentiments pour ta punition.*
>
> (927–28)

In blank verse, the echo of the lines is not effective enough to justify the obvious repetition—and so John C. Lapp simply renders the first couplet as

> But this you must not ask, that I renounce
> My worthy act in cowardly repentance.

—followed later by Chimène's lines—

> Yet this you must not ask, that I renounce
> For love of you, my claim that you be punished.

In fact, the irony of the precise echo can only be driven home (or recalled) through rhyme:

> RODRIGUE: For you must not expect me to retract,
> Despite my love for you, a righteous act.

—echoed later by Chimène's

> And you must not expect me to retract,
> Despite my love for you, this vengeful act.

A related mnemonic characteristic of Cornelian drama is that its language is loaded with memorable maxims, with "quotable quotes"; the use of rhymed couplets lends itself to such neat, crisp, and well-turned formulations, sealed by an affirming ring which makes the line memorable (as well as rememberable). Often, the first line of the couplet sets up the consequent maxim, as in Don Diègue's lines to Rodrigue in 1.5:

> *Ne réplique point, je connais ton amour;*
> *Mais qui peut vivre infâme est indigne du jour.*
> (283–84)[21]

Pope discovered and illustrated the same facility for epigrammatic proverbs in his use of the English couplet: "True wit is Nature to advantage dressed, / What oft was thought, but ne'er so well expressed"; or "Good nature and good sense must ever join; / To err is human, to forgive divine." The mnemonic key of rhyme locks and seals the compact verbal formulation of the semantic idea into the listener's memory file, with a precision and ordered neatness that allows for easy mental recall.

This effect is clearly dissipated in blank verse. For example, when the Infante explains to Léonor (523–26: 2.5)—

> *Ah! qu'avec peu d'effet on entend la raison,*
> *Quand le coeur est atteint d'un si charmant poison!*
> *Et lorsque le malade aime sa maladie,*
> *Qu'il a peine à souffrir que l'on y remédie!*

—the latter couplet strikes the ear with the ring of a universal truth, easily applicable and quotable in other contexts. Mr. Cairncross's blank verse is quite competent here, but cannot manage the epigrammatic quality:

> How ineffectively does reason curb
> The heart a magic potion acts upon.
> And, when the patient loves the malady,
> How hard he finds it to permit the cure.

Only rhyme provides the satisfaction of tidy conclusiveness:

> With what little effect one heeds the will
> Of reason when such charming poisons fill
> One's heart! When sick men love their maladies,
> They suffer most when they find remedies.

Similarly, the opening couplet of 3.5 is a clearly universal maxim, spoken by Don Diègue:

> *Jamais nous ne goûtons de parfaite allegresse;*
> *Nos plux heureux succès sont mêlés de tristesse.*
> *Toujours quelques soucis en ces événements*
> *Troublent la pureté de nos contentements.*

(1001–4)

Mr. Cairncross's

> We never taste a bliss that's unalloyed.
> Sadness attends our happiest success.

is unable to distinguish the tenor of these lines from the rest of his blank verse. Again, only strictly end-stopping rhyming lines can sound as neatly wrought:

> We never taste a perfect happiness,
> But find some sorrow inside each success.
> Some problems always mar the purity,
> In these events, of our felicity.

Clearly, then, we want the flourish of the final rhyme when it is called for. But at the same time we cannot allow an unmitigated succession of fireworks, lest the memorable maxim or flourishing finale be lost in indistinguishable monotony. As in all verse drama, much of the body of verse must flow smoothly and inconspicuously, delivering its contents in the sort of transparent verse paragraphs to which blank verse is so admirably suited. Therefore, in a translation which requires the logic and control of couplets, it is nevertheless important in many passages to mute the clanging bell of rhyme, so that a verse paragraph does not break down into a series of boring and predictable jingles. To that purpose, I have applied the same verse-paragraph techniques that blank verse uses to mute the strict, five-stress, ten-syllable, end-stopped line. First of all, we can make frequent use of enjamb-ment (run-on lines). We can also mitigate the singsong iambic five-count by breaking up lines with internal pauses, so that the system of syntactical pauses cuts across the grain of line-patterns. We can further vary the number of strong stresses in each line, so that the lines do not produce a uniform, metronomic beat. Finally, we can employ trochees, "scudded" feet (to use Nabokov's term for pyrrhic feet), elision, and polysyllabic words (or spon-dees for an opposite effect) to make a line skim quickly on a succession of unaccented syllables:

> The multitúd'nous séas incárnadine.

As an example of the verse-paragraph effect, with occasionally more obvious rhymes when called for, here is my translation of the play's *récit*, Rodrigue's narrative recitation of offstage action:

> The dim light of the stars at last unveils
> To sight upon the tide some thirty sails;
> The waves form, lifting both the Moors and sea
> Up to the harbor jointly. Quietly
> We let the Moors pass by; all seems asleep;
> No soldiers anywhere in sight; our deep
> Silence deceives their minds: how could they doubt
> But that they had surprised us? So without
> Fear they approach, cast anchor, disembark—
> Right in our waiting hands there in the dark.
> We then rise up, and, all at once, let fly
> A thousand thunderous cries up to the sky.
> At this, our men in ships shout their replies,
> And come out armed. Confused by all the cries,
> The Moors are seized with fear as they alight,
> Thinking they've lost ere they've begun to fight.
> They came for pillage, only to find war;
> We press them hard, both on the sea and shore,
> Make their blood run in rivulets before
> They can resist or form their ranks once more.
>   But soon, in spite of us, they're rallied by
> Their kings; courage returns, their fear to die
> Dispelled: the shame of death without a fight
> Restores their courage, discipline, and might.
> They face us firmly and flash their scimitars,
> Horribly mingling into their blood ours.
> The earth, the fleet, the river and the port
> Are fields of carnage, where Death keeps his court.

(O!) How many deeds, how many a brilliant fight
Go without notice in the dark of night,
Where each man sees but his own mighty blows,
And which way Fate will fall, none of them knows!
I move about, encouraging our men,
Advancing or regrouping them, and when
Others arrive, I lead them to the fray,
Not knowing the outcome till the break of day.
The dawn shows our advantage, finally:
The Moors see they are lost, and suddenly
Lose heart; seeing our reinforcements nigh,
Their will to win cedes to their fear to die.
They reach their ships, and cut the cables, crying
Frightfully up to the sky, while flying
In frenzied haste, without considering
Where their kings are, or what is happening
To them. Their fright's too strong for loyalty:
Brought by the tide, now the ebb takes them to sea,
While yet their kings, and some few of their men,
All wounded by our blows, fight even then,
Selling their lives quite dearly, valiantly.
It is in vain I bid them yield to me:
Scimitars clutched, they choose to ignore my call
At first; but seeing all their soldiers fall
By their feet they concede they've lost the field,
And ask for leaders—I step forth—they yield
To me. . . .

                                                      (1273–1327)

The final test of any translation into English, of course, is that it be *readable* as English—in the case of a play, that it be readable as drama. Specifically, the test with *Le Cid* is for the simultaneous maintenance of lofty tone and rhetoric, rhymed couplets, *and* stageable dialogue. For such a test, let us look at my translation of act 2, scene 1, a rather ordinary scene in which the Count (Chimène's father), having just insulted Don Diègue (Rodrigue's father), has a conversation with another nobleman of the king's court, Don Arias. Ultimately, the reader (or audience) must be the sole judge of the failure or success of any literary or dramatic endeavor:

Act 2, Scene 1
(A chamber in the palace: Don Arias, the Count)

THE COUNT: I was a bit hot-headed, I admit,
          And in my anger went too far; but it
          Is past and done, there is no remedy.

DON ARIAS: Submit your pride to the King's will, for he
              Is angry and concerned, and may, it's true,
              Use full authority to punish you.
              Besides, you have no tenable defense;
              The victim's rank and that of the offense
              Demand submissions, as your obligations
              Go beyond ordinary reparations.

THE COUNT: The king may do with me what suits his whim.

DON ARIAS: You are too proud when you speak thus of him.
              Go and appease him now—he loves you still.
              Surely you would not disobey his will?

THE COUNT: When questions of esteem, sir, come along,
              Some disobedience is no great wrong.
              And if it's wrong, my service to the King
              Exonerates me, or should, of anything.

DON ARIAS: However great one's deeds and glory be,
              A king is never bound to such as we.
              Flatter yourself no more, sir; they who serve
              The King, you should well know, do but observe
              Their duty. Your approach, sir, cannot win.

THE COUNT: When I have tried I'll know how wrong I've been.

DON ARIAS: You'd best respect the power of a king.

THE COUNT: Even the King cannot in one day bring
              My doom, despite the power at his call.
              If I should fall, then all Castile will fall.

DON ARIAS: What! You dare think the sovereign power could not—

THE COUNT: The King needs me. He knows, because I fought
              For him and saved his realm and his renown,
              That should my head fall, he would lose his crown.

DON ARIAS: Heed my advice, and let yourself be guided
              By reason.

THE COUNT: There's no need. I have decided.

DON ARIAS: What word should I report, then, to the King?

THE COUNT: That I will not be shamed in anything.

DON ARIAS: But kings demand a power that's absolute.

THE COUNT: The die is cast and I am resolute.

DON ARIAS: Adieu, then. But your laurels cannot spare
             Your head from harm when lightning strikes—beware.

THE COUNT: I'll wait without fear.

DON ARIAS: That won't change the action.

THE COUNT: Well, then, Don Diegue may get his satisfaction.
             (Exit Don Arias)
             No threats can daunt me; I've no fear of death.
             I'll weather any storms while I have breath.
             I might be forced to live in misery,
             But without honor life is death for me.

   In conclusion, I believe that, while the difficulties to be surmounted in rhymed translation are formidable, they are *not* impossible—and, once done, the benefits in both stylistic effect and fidelity are considerable. The challenges (and risk of failure) in rhymed translation are great; but one can, and should try, to have it all. In so trying, one weds Romantic drive with Classical discipline.

   In the end, however, one must admit that any translation must fall far short of the original, and it is with frustration that I compare a lovely, witty, or perfectly formed Corneille couplet with my corresponding translation. Given the intentions of "faithfulness" I had in writing my translation and the set of rigorous difficulties imposed on it, I certainly could not but fall short, as all translators must, in any scrupulous comparison with the original; any serious reader of French should not deny himself the beauty of the original text. Still, for the translator the activity is a labor of love and pleasure.[22] While I cannot deny the partial and inevitable truth in Robert Frost's oft-quoted comment that "Poetry is what is lost in translation," still there is unquestionably pleasure and satisfaction in fashioning a crisp and well-turned couplet, in the exultation of having, at least for the moment, sur-mounted the difficulties with a controlled grace. That is the classical aspiration, and the challenge which the rhyming translator must undertake. And then one can always at least add to whatever small or limited success one attains the consolation that (in the words of Don Diègue):

> *Jamais nous ne goûtons de parfaite allegresse. . . .*
> ("We never taste a perfect happiness"—line 1001.)

Notes on the Translation

1. There are several recurrent words or idioms whose usage and meaning in the French I have kept: (a) "Lover" *(amant)* is used, not in the modern sense, but in the sense of "my lover, my true love." Similarly, "mistress" *(maîtresse)* has no illicit or extramarital implications. (b) To "pursue" *(pour-suivre)* a person (or his crime, his death, his valor, and so on) means to seek one's revenge, to receive satisfaction from him, usually through his death; to "pursue a lover" does *not* mean to flirt or chase after someone. (c) The words "offend" and "offense" *(offenser)* are used, as in the French, to mean insult, outrage, dishonor, and so forth—and not in the sense implied by the word "offensive," meaning repulsive (as in "offend one's taste"). (d) A recurring rhyme in the play is the rhyme of *Chimène* with *peine;* I have preserved the rhyming of "Chimene" with "pain" because it occurs so frequently in the original, and is so fitting in context. I am sure there are numerous other preservations of French meaning or usage, but the above are perhaps the ones most requiring explanation. (Chapter 3 discusses in greater detail the concepts and conventions of French classical drama.)

2. As in the French tradition, the strict syllable count is dependent on numerous *liaisons:* these elisions, contractions, and syncopes are, I hope, quite obvious to sight and sound in the metrical context, and I have made no particular effort to point them out typographically—thus, "against" might be read " 'gainst," "ever" might be read "e'er," "misery is" might be read "misery_is," "honorable" might be "hon'rable," "to avenge" might be "to_avenge," "I see it" might be "I see't."

3. In two or three instances, a parenthesized expletive *(Ah!* or *O!)* occurs: when parenthesized, it is meant to be an exclamation, a sigh, or an aside, and not part of the line's metrical scheme.

4. And finally, in a translation there is always a tension between writing what sounds more like English and being faithful to the particular French word, metaphor, image, or idiom. I have tried to satisfy both aims where possible, sometimes keeping a French word or image whose usage may not be native to English, sometimes rendering an equivalent English expression or idea.

Le Cid

A Translation in Rhymed Couplets

Dramatis Personae

DON FERNAND	first king of Castile.
THE INFANTE	Doña Urraque, daughter of the King.
DON DIEGUE	father of Don Rodrigue.
THE COUNT	Don Gomes, Count of Gormas, father of Chimene.
DON RODRIGUE	lover of Chimene.
DON SANCHE	suitor to Chimene.
DON ARIAS	Castilian nobleman.
DON ALONSE	Castilian nobleman.
CHIMENE	daughter of the Count.
LEONOR	governess of the Infante.
ELVIRE	governess of Chimene.
PAGE	the Infante's page.

The scene is set in Seville, by the Guadalquivir River.

Le Cid

ACT 1

Scene 1——CHIMENE, ELVIRE
(At Chimene's house)

CHIMENE

Elvire, is your report completely true?
What did my father really say to you?

ELVIRE

I'm still savoring your prospects of success:
You love Rodrique; your father does no less.
5   To Rodrigue's love, if I should guess his pleasure,
He bids you to respond in equal measure.

CHIMENE

Oh, tell me again, I pray you, line by line,
What makes you think his choice agrees with mine.
Repeat those magic words of hope to me—
10   Such words cannot be heard too frequently.
My heart will never tire to hear you say
That it may bare its passion in plain day,
And choose to bow at Don Rodrigue's command.
Of these two suitors vying for my hand,

15 Don Sanche and Don Rodrigue—did you not make
    My father see which one I hope he'll take?

    No, no: quite neutral I portrayed you, neither
    Inflating nor destroying hope for either,
    Not solemn and not frivolous, but rather,
20 Eager to heed the choice of your dear father.
    He was touched; instantly there came a glow
    Of pride in his warm glance, pleased at this show
    Of your devotion. Since you wish, I see,
    To hear it once more, here's what he said to me:
25 "She behaves rightly. Both are men of worth,
    Being of noble and loyal blood by birth,
    Both young, but in their eyes I plainly see
    The valiant spirit of their ancestry.
    Rodrigue's features, especially, reveal
30 The embodiment of the heroic ideal—
    A worthy son of a long lineage
    Teeming with mighty heroes, age to age.
    His father's courage, at one time, surpassed
    Human belief, wondrous to see; at last
35 Age etched his exploits on his brow to give
    Hint of the type of life a man can live.
    This courage lives still in the son; so tell
    Chimene that she may love—it suits me well."
    Having but scarce begun, he was cut short
40 As the King's Council called, and off to Court
    He went; but by his several words I find
    That toward Rodrigue he's favorably inclined.
    The King must choose a tutor for his son:
    Surely your father is the only one
45 Who by his peerless valor can make claim
    To such a place of great honor and fame.
    His claim is just, for his high deeds will voice
    His merit, and ensure him the King's choice.
    Since Rodrigue's father shall, when that is done,
50 Propose the match desired by his son,
    Your father will bring good news—and you will see
    How soon your hopes become reality.

CHIMENE

It seems my troubled heart, never content,
Cannot accept such joy, but is intent
55 On seeing darker sides; indeed I fear
That soon this hour of joy may disappear.

ELVIRE

Your fears will vanish on this very day.

CHIMENE

Well, we shall wait and see, let come what may.

THE INFANTE

Page, go inform Chimene that she is late
60   In seeing me today, and as I hate
Slothfulness, tell her not to make delay.

(Exit page)

LEONOR

Madame, the same desire every day
Eats at your heart: you wish to inquire of her
The state of her relations with her lover.

THE INFANTE

65   Not without reason. It was I who brought
Chimene before Love's shrine, and I who taught
Rodrigue to woo her, conquering her scorn;
In short, it was through me their love was born.
Thus, having shackled them in lovers' chains,
70   Shouldn't I try to see them through Love's pains?

LEONOR

Madame, you always show too much chagrin
At the good fortune they find themselves in.
Why should the happy love between these two
Cause such deep misery and pain for you?
75   Why should your great concern for them destory
Your peace of mind, when it brings them such joy?
But I forget myself, and lack of discretion.

THE INFANTE

Secrecy only increases my depression:
So let me tell you how my heart has fought
80   Against Love's many cruel assaults. I'm caught
In its unsparing tyranny and sway:
This knight, this lover whom I give away,
I love—

LEONOR

You love him!

THE INFANTE *(taking Leonor's hand)*

                    Feel my heart beat faster
And flutter at the mention of its master;
85 It knows him.

LEONOR

            Forgive me, Madame, if I
Speak openly, to say this love must die.
How could a princess like yourself lose sight
Of her own place, and love a common knight?
How would the King, and all Castile, react?
90 You are his daughter; don't forget that fact.

THE INFANTE

I'd rather die than fall into disgrace
And stoop so low as to deny my place.
I might reply that, in the noblest hearts,
Merit alone should serve for Cupid's darts;
95 If my desire had need of an excuse,
There are a thousand precedents it could use.
But I'll defend the glory of my station,
And fight desire with determination.
Only a monarch, I am well aware,
100 Has worth enough to wed a royal heir
Such as I am. So, for my weak heart's sake,
I gave to another what I dared not take:
He loves Chimene instead; I lit the fires
Of love in them to quench my own desires.
105 No wonder my tormented heart attends
The announcement of their wedding, and depends
On that to help restore my inner peace.
Love thrives on hope, but dies when all hopes cease,
Its flames put out for lack of sustenance.
110 Despite the pains of my sad circumstance,
When these two lovers are securely wed,
My spirit is healed, because my hope is dead.

Meanwhile I suffer, and my soul is torn,
For yet Rodrigue lies near my heart; I'm sworn
115 To lose him, but with much regretfulness—
And there's the cause of my unhappiness.
Sadly I see how Love has brought me pain,
Making me sigh for whom I must disdain.
My spirit's split by honor and desire:
120 Although my will is strong, my heart's on fire.
The fateful marriage I both crave and dread
Can be but a mixed joy to heart or head.
Both honor and love tug at my soul; and so
I live in pain, whether they wed or no.

LEONOR

125 Madame, what can I say, except to add
My sympathy; just now, it's true, I had
Blamed you—I should have pitied you instead.
But since you fight a force both dear and dread—
Parrying its sweet kiss, its powerful arms,
130 Repulsing its assaults, its tender charms—
Trust virtue and honor to restore your peace
Of mind; rest all your hopes in them, and cease
To worry. Time and faith in God will bring
An end to all your hapless suffering.

THE INFANTE

135 My greatest hope is but to hope no more.

PAGE *(reentering)*

Chimene is here at your request.

THE INFANTE

Leonor,
Go entertain her in the gallery.

LEONOR

While you remain in futile revery?

THE INFANTE

I just need time to calm my anguished state
140 And look composed, despite my troubled fate.
I'll follow you.
      (Alone)   Lord God, source of salvation,
Please put an end to my great tribulation.
Secure my honor, and my peace of mind.
Let me, in the joy of others, *my* joy find.
145 This marriage affects three souls equally:
Let it take place, and You shall set me free.
Join these two lovers in holy ecstasy;
Release me from my chains and agony.
But I delay; I'll see Chimene, and pray
150 Her visit helps to end my pains today.

SCENE 3——THE COUNT, DON DIEGUE
(A public square outside the royal palace)

THE COUNT

You've won now—the King's favor raises you
To a rank which but to me alone is due:
The tutor to the young prince of Castile.

DON DIEGUE

This honor to my family, I feel,
155 Proves to the world he's fair, and promises
A just reward for all past services.

THE COUNT

Great as kings are, they're only men, and can
Be just as wrong as any common man.
The King's choice proves to all his partialness:
160 There's no reward for present services.

DON DIEGUE

Let's not speak of a choice which vexes you:
Favor instead of merit might, it's true,
Have been his motive. But one must abide,
Without examining, what kings decide.
165 There's yet another honor which I crave:
That we be joined by a holy bond. You have
Only one daughter, I've a single son;
We could be friends and our two houses one
If you'd accept Rodrigue as son-in-law.

THE COUNT

170 He may not deign to be my son-in-law
If, swelled with pride at your new dignity,
He aims much higher in his vanity.
Instruct the Prince, Monsieur, and show him how
To rule a nation, make the people bow
175 Before the law, be loved by virtuous and
True men, and make the wicked fear his hand.

Add to these virtues those of soldiership:
Show the Prince how to endure intense hardship,
Become unrivaled in the martial art,
180 Spend days on horseback without losing heart,
Sleep in his armor, scale a fortress wall,
With victory in war his all-in-all.
Teach by example, and his skill perfect;
Teach him by acts, that he see their effect.

DON DIEGUE

185 To learn by acts, despite your jealousy,
He needs only to read my history,
My life: the sequence of my feats will show
How one must rule a nation, let him know
How to attack, how to draw up and lead
190 An army, and build his fame on act and deed.

THE COUNT

A live example would much better teach
The Prince his duties than a book, and each
Day of my life is, after all, by far
More glorious than all your back pages are.
195 If you were brave once, I today am more
Valiant. My strong arm serves as buttress for
Our kingdom. Aragon and Granada quake
With fear at my name; thus, when I but shake
My sword, Castile is safe. Without my sword,
200 We'd waste our lives under a foreign lord
And foreign laws. Each day, each moment sees
More glorious praise for my great victories.
Under my own protection, at my side,
The Prince could test his valor: he could ride
205 Into a battle, and learn to conquer nations
By my example. With such preparations,
He—

DON DIEGUE

Yes, yes, I know how commendably
You've served the King: you once fought under me.
When old age filled my veins with ice, your brave

210 Spirit was there to take my place and save
The kingdom. To be brief, you are today
What I was yesteryear. Yet, let me say
That by his choice it seems the King can find
Some difference between us in his mind.

THE COUNT

215 You stole the honor I deserve from me.

DON DIEGUE

The man who wins deserves it—only he.

THE COUNT

The post should go to him who'd be of use.

DON DIEGUE

That man's unworthy whom monarchs refuse.

THE COUNT

You won the post through courtier's influence.

DON DIEGUE

220 My reputation was my sole defense.

THE COUNT

Or was it just the King's respect for age?

DON DIEGUE

Courage came first: this honor was my wage.

THE COUNT

In terms of courage, I deserve it most.

DON DIEGUE

He who has lost does not deserve the post.

THE COUNT

225   I don't deserve? I?

DON DIEGUE

You.

THE COUNT

Such impudence,
You bold dotard, will have its recompense.
        (He slaps Don Diegue)

DON DIEGUE

                (His hand on his sword)
Now kill me, then, for none of my old race
Has ever suffered such a cruel disgrace.
        (They struggle)

THE COUNT

Do you mean—weak old fool—to fight indeed?

DON DIEGUE

230   Oh God! my strength deserts me in my need!
        (The Count disarms him)

THE COUNT

I have your sword; but take it back, lest you
Take pride in being disarmed by me. Adieu.
Go bid the Prince, despite my jealousy,
To heed you well, and read the history
235   Of your life: there he'll learn that insolence
In old fools merits a just recompense.
                        (Exit the Count)

SCENE 4——DON DIEGUE

DON DIEGUE *(alone)*

Rage and despair at old, despisèd age!
Is infamy the theme of life's last page?
I've served the King too well in every way
240   To see my honor wither in a day!
My arm, which Spain respects and men admire,
My arm, the former savior of the empire,
How could you, once the power behind the throne,
Betray me when I need you most? I've grown
245   Too old; this arm's a relic now; can all
The hard-won honor of a lifetime fall
In one day? New rank, source of my disgrace,
High peak from which I fall to this low place,
Must I endure this insult to my name,
250   Die unrevenged, or dare to live in shame?
No, Count, *you* tutor the young Prince for now.
Such a high rank as that cannot allow
For a dishonored, broken man like me:
I'm proved unfit through your proud jealousy.
255   This, my sword, once a glorious instrument,
Is but a bloodless old man's ornament.
Once so respected, it could not prevent
My loss of honor in this argument.   *(Looking at the sword)*
Then you must pass to stronger hands that *can*
260   Avenge me—I'm a miserable old man.

SCENE 5——DON DIEGUE, RODRIGUE

(Enter Rodrigue)

DON DIEGUE

Rodrigue, speak: are you brave?

RODRIGUE

I'll send him who
Dares doubt it to his grave.

DON DIEGUE

Well said! Such true
Resolve is music to my troubled ears.
The family spirit thrives in you and nears
265   The proud perfection of my younger days.
Come, then, my son, my blood, and earn my praise,
Come and avenge me.

RODRIGUE

Of what?

DON DIEGUE

Of my shame,
A mortal blow dishonoring our name:
A slap. I would have killed him, but old age
270   Baffled my noble urge. This cruel outrage
Must be avenged, and since my arm no longer
Can wield this sword, I give it to your stronger
Arm to avenge. Go challenge him and trust
Your courage against his arrogance: you must
275   Kill or be killed, for blood alone can free
Our pride. I'll be direct—your enemy
Is to be feared: I've seen him, bloody and aching,
Intimidate entire armies, breaking
Through scores of squadrons by sheer bravery.
280   But that's not all: I must tell you that he
Is more than just a valiant soldier—rather,
He's . . .

RODRIGUE

Please, get to the point.

DON DIEGUE

He's Chimene's father.

RODRIGUE

He's—

DON DIEGUE

Yes, I know your love—so don't reply;
But live in shame and you deserve to die.
285 The more that the offender's dear to you,
The greater his offense. Vengeance is due,
You know it. Avenge me and avenge yourself;
Prove worthy of a father like myself.
Crushed by the curse of fate, my spirits bow
290 Like willows. Go, run, fly—avenge us now!

(Exit Don Diegue)

SCENE 6———RODRIGUE

RODRIGUE *(alone)*

Oh, struck deep in my heart
By a cruel blow unlooked for and acute,
Wretched avenger in a just dispute,
Unwilling pawn, yet bound to play the part,
295   I remain rooted, and my troubled soul
          Has lost control.
     So close to having Chimene's hand—
         Oh God, what pain!
     The victim is my father, and
300   The offender, father of Chimene.

     Harsh and unjust demand!
It pits my honor against my love; to obey
A father, I must throw my love away.
One spurs my pride, the other stays my hand.
305   My choice is whether to betray love's flame,
         Or live in shame;
     Both ways I'm cursed forevermore.
        Oh God, the pain!
     Should I neglect my honor, or
310   Punish the father of Chimene?

     Should duty, or love, hold sway?
I'm bound by just yet difficult constraints:
Either my pleasure is gone, or pleasure taints
My name, unworthy of the light of day.   *(Looks at the sword)*
315   You dear yet cruel hope of a noble heart
         That's torn apart
     By love—fair foe of happiness,
         You bring me pain:
     Is it to spur my vengefulness?
320   Is it to make me lose Chimene?

     Death might best end my pain.
My duty is also to Chimene: this path
Of vengeance would incur her hate and wrath.
But to refrain would merit her disdain.
325   Either I prove unfaithful, or a lover

Unworthy of her.
Everything seems, whatever I try,
To increase my pain.
Come now, my soul: since we must die,
330   At least let's not offend Chimene.

To die thus unrevenged!
And bring our family name such infamy!
All Spain would impute to my memory
The stigma of a house left unavenged!
335   To seek a love which necessarily
Is lost to me!
Heed such seductive thoughts no more—
They bring you pain.
Salvage, at least, your honor, for,
340   In any case you'll lose Chimene.

Yes, love has blinded me.
My duty's to my father: I'll defend
The honor of our blood, whether I end
My life in combat or in misery.
345   I move too slow! I must run to my fate,
Not hesitate;
Ashamed by such deliberation,
I'll end my pain
Avenging this humiliation
350   Wrought by the father of Chimene.

ACT 2

SCENE 1——DON ARIAS, THE COUNT
(A chamber in the palace)

THE COUNT

I was a bit hot-headed, I admit,
And in my anger went too far; but it
Is past and done, there is no remedy.

DON ARIAS

Submit your pride to the King's will, for he
355 Is angry and concerned, and may, it's true
Use full authority to punish you.
Besides, you have no tenable defense;
The victim's rank and that of the offense
Demand submissions, as your obligations
360 Go beyond ordinary reparations.

THE COUNT

The King may do with me what suits his whim.

DON ARIAS

You are too proud when you speak thus of him.
Go and appease him now; he loves you still.
Surely you would not disobey his will?

THE COUNT

365 When questions of esteem, sir, come along,
Some disobedience is no great wrong.
And if it's wrong, my service to the King
Exonerates me, or should, of anything.

DON ARIAS

However great one's deeds and glory be,
370   A king is never bound to such as we.
Flatter yourself no more, sir; they who serve
The King, you should well know, do but observe
Their duty. Your approach, sir, cannot win.

THE COUNT

When I have tried I'll know how wrong I've been.

DON ARIAS

375   You'd best respect the power of a king.

THE COUNT

Even the King cannot in one day bring
My doom, despite the power at his call.
If I should fall, then all Castile will fall.

DON ARIAS

What! You dare think the sovereign power could not—

THE COUNT

380   The King needs me. He knows, because I fought
For him and saved his realm and his renown,
That should my head fall, he would lose his crown.

DON ARIAS

Heed my advice, and let yourself be guided
By reason.

THE COUNT

There's no need. I have decided.

DON ARIAS

385   What word should I report, then, to the King?

THE COUNT

That I will not be shamed in anything.

DON ARIAS

But kings demand a power that's absolute.

THE COUNT

The die is cast and I am resolute.

DON ARIAS

Adieu, then. But your laurels cannot spare
390   Your head from harm when lightning strikes—beware.

THE COUNT

I'll wait without fear.

DON ARIAS

That won't change the action.

THE COUNT

Well, then, Don Diegue may get his satisfaction.
    (Exit Don Arias; the Count alone)
No threats can daunt me, I've no fear of death.
I'll weather any storms while I have breath.
395   I might be forced to live in misery,
But without honor life is death for me. — Same for women

SCENE 2———THE COUNT, DON RODRIGUE

(Enter Rodrigue)

RODRIGUE

A word with you, Count.

THE COUNT

Speak.

RODRIGUE

Resolve my doubt.

You know Don Diegue?

THE COUNT

I do.

RODRIGUE

Softly—don't shout.

He was, of all the men that ever sat

400   Beside the King, the truest—you know that?

THE COUNT

Perhaps.

RODRIGUE

The fiery color in my stare

Is his blood—you know that?

THE COUNT

Why should I care?

RODRIGUE

I'll show you why, if you'll just step outside.

THE COUNT

Presumptuous youth!

RODRIGUE

          Be calm, and try to hide
405   These passions. Though I'm young, my noble birth
Makes up for age in bravery and worth.

THE COUNT

Compare yourself to me! What vanity,
In one as yet untried as you must be!

RODRIGUE

Men like myself don't need a second test.
410   My maiden strokes will match those of the best.

THE COUNT

Do you know who I am?

RODRIGUE

             Yes; other men
May shudder merely at your name, and when
They see your head covered with laurel, say   *fearless to death*
Death at your hands will be my fate today.
415   But still I dare challenge your martial art.
I'll find enough strength, having enough heart.
For vengeance' sake, nothing's impossible;
You're undefeated, not invincible.

THE COUNT

Your speech reveals the great courage which I
420   Have oft observed in you. In your heart lie
The honor and the spirit of our Spain;
Thus, I was pleased to choose you for Chimene.
I know your love: and I am glad to find
That it is ruled by duty, that your mind
425   Preserves your honor, unimpaired by love.   *✦ imp: that duty &*
honor come before
love.

Your admirable valor is above
Description. As I want the perfect knight
For son-in-law, I'm sure I chose the right
Young man. I sympathize with you, in truth,
430   Admire your courage, and lament your youth.
Don't seek a fatal first encounter, spare
My strength from such an unequal affair.
I'd gain no honor through this victory,
No glory, since there is no risk for me.
435   They'll say I won with ease, a worthless prize—
And I'd be left regretting your demise.

RODRIGUE

These cowardly qualms reveal your inner strife:
You took my pride, yet fear to take my life?

THE COUNT

Away with you!

RODRIGUE

Let's go—not waste our breath.

THE COUNT

440   You want to live?

RODRIGUE

Are you afraid of death?

THE COUNT

Come, then! since it's your duty; you debase
Don Diegue if you survive his deep disgrace.

SCENE 3——THE INFANTE, CHIMENE, LEONOR
(The Infante's house)

THE INFANTE

Allay your sorrow, dear Chimene, and be
Steadfast through this misfortune. You will see
445   A calm follow this feeble storm; your bliss
Is masked but by a passing cloud; you'll miss
Nothing to have your joy slightly delayed.

CHIMENE

My heart's too troubled to hope or be allayed.
This sudden storm now breaks on the calm sea,
450   Portending certain shipwreck; surely we
Will perish before leaving port. I loved,
I was beloved; our fathers both approved.
While I was telling you this heaven-sent
News, they began their wretched argument,
455   The sad tidings of which, no sooner brought,
Dashed all my hopes—my sweet dreams came to naught.
Cursèd ambition, detestable madness,
Tyrants who bring the noblest spirits sadness!
Unmerciful pride, foe to my dearest goal,
460   How many tears and sighs you'll cost my soul!

THE INFANTE

This quarrel gives you no real cause to fear:
Quickly begun, it will quickly disappear.
It has caused too much stir, and will soon end;
The King himself wants peace. I am your friend,
465   Chimene, and sympathize; anything I
Can do to end this quarrel I will try.

CHIMENE

This case can have no reconciliation.
Such deep affronts are beyond reparation.
Reason and force are useless. Though outside
470   Wounds may seem healed, the hate that they may hide
Deep in their hearts, remains a flame forever,
Burning in secret, but as fiercely as ever.

THE INFANTE

Their two children will very soon be tied
By holy bonds, making them put aside
475   Their hatred. Love, you'll see, will prove to be
Stronger than hate, restoring harmony.

CHIMENE

I wish it, but my hopes are few: I know
My father; and Don Diegue's too proud. Tears flow
In spite of me—I can scarce hide my sorrow;
480   The past torments me, and I fear the morrow.

THE INFANTE

You fear an old man's feebleness and rage?

CHIMENE

Rodrigue has courage.

THE INFANTE

But he lacks in age.

CHIMENE

Men who are valiant are so from the first.

THE INFANTE

You need not fear him, though. He's too immersed
485   In his great love for you to cross your path,
And one word from your lips would end his wrath.

CHIMENE

What agony, if he should not obey!
But if he should, what would all Castile say?
For him to bear such an indignity!
490   Whether he yield or not to his love for me,
I either feel shame for his weaker side,
Or pain at his denial, though justified.

THE INFANTE

Your noble soul, though much involved, cannot
Admit a single, low, unworthy thought.
495 But if until a settlement occur,
This perfect lover I make my prisoner,
And keep him from displaying his bravery,
Then will your heart feel less anxiety?

CHIMENE

Ah! Then, Madame, I'd have no cause to fear.

SCENE 4——THE INFANTE, CHIMENE, LEONOR, PAGE
(Enter page)

THE INFANTE

500 Page, go seek out Rodrigue, and bring him here.

PAGE

Madame, the Count and he—

CHIMENE

Oh, God! I fear—

THE INFANTE

Go on . . .

PAGE

Together just went out of here.

THE INFANTE

Alone?

PAGE

Yes, seemingly in hushed contention.

CHIMENE

They fight! Let's speak no more; your good intention
505 Comes too late. Please, Madame, forgive my hurry.
(Exit Chimene)

SCENE 5——THE INFANTE, LEONOR

THE INFANTE

Alas! What anguish fills my soul! I worry
And feel for her, but Rodrigue thrills my heart.
My peace has left me, and my passions start
To thrive once more. Rodrigue's break with Chimene
510 Brings both my hopes and pain to life again.
Though I regret their separation, still
My inner spirit feels a secret thrill.

LEONOR

What! Does this shameful passion in your soul
So soon defeat its noble self-control?

THE INFANTE

515 Don't call it shameful: in my heart it reigns
Triumphant and majestic now. Take pains
To respect something that's so dear to me.
Although my honor fights it, still I see
That my weak heart has a mad hope, and flies
520 After Rodrigue, now that Chimene's love dies.

LEONOR

So thus you let your noble courage fail,
And thus now reason is of no avail?

THE INFANTE

With what little effect one heeds the will
Of reason when such charming poisons fill
525 One's heart! When sick men love their maladies,
They suffer most when they find remedies.

LEONOR

Hope has deceived you, and has marred your view:
Madame, Rodrigue is not worthy of you.

THE INFANTE

I know it all too well; but should I start
530 To yield, learn how my love beguiles my heart:
If Rodrigue wins the duel, causing the fall
Of this great warrior through his might, then all
Is possible: I could love him without shame.
If he defeats the Count, what could you name
535 That he can't do? I dare imagine him
Conquering entire kingdoms at his whim,
And my deceiving heart convinces me
I see him on Granada's throne, and see
The Moors, defeated, trembling in great dread
540 Of him, Aragon hailing its new head,
Portugal surrendering, his victories
Bearing his famed laurels across the seas,
Washed in the blood of Africans. In brief,
After this victory, it's my belief
545 He'll be a warrior of the first degree
And prove full worthy to be loved by me.

LEONOR

But, Madame, watch how far you praise his might,
Which still depends on whether or not they fight.

THE INFANTE

Rodrigue's outraged; the Count admits the deed;
550 They left together: what more do you need?

LEONOR

All right! They fight, since you would have it so;
But will Rodrigue go as far as *you* now go?

THE INFANTE

What can I say? I'm mad, my mind's at sea:
You see what evils love prepares for me.
555 Come to my chamber, and console my pain;
Don't leave me while in anguish I remain.

SCENE 6——DON FERNAND, DON ARIAS, DON SANCHE
(At the Court of Don Fernand)

DON FERNAND *(The King)*

Impossible man! Does he expect to be
Pardoned for this offense? What vanity!

DON ARIAS

     I spoke with him at length on your behalf;
560 I tried my best, Sir, but his ears were deaf.

DON FERNAND

Good heavens! Does an audacious vassal so
Little respect me now as first to go
Insult Don Diegue, and then to scorn his king?
In my own Court will he rule everything!
565 Brave warrior and great captain though he be,
I know well how to tame such vanity.
Were he valor itself, or god of great
Warriors, I'd make him learn a rebel's fate.
Despite his insolence, I had still meant
570 To show him leniency. But since he went
So far as to abuse it, act now: go
Arrest him, whether he resist or no.

DON SANCHE

Sir, Time might make him more obedient:
He is still fuming from the argument;
575 A noble soul cannot yield easily
When still so hot with anger. He can see
He's in the wrong, but such a lofty heart
Cannot so soon admit the guilty part.

DON FERNAND

Keep quiet, Don Sanche, and be now notified
580 You share his guilt if you dare take his side.

DON SANCHE

I beg you, Sir, although I will obey,
A word in his defense.

DON FERNAND

What could you say?

DON SANCHE

That one accustomed to great acts cannot
Lower himself to the debasing thought
585 Of such submission without feeling shame:
That's what he fears, and that's what is to blame.
He finds his duty a bit too harsh: he'd start
To obey you were he not so great of heart.
Order his arm, nourished by valiant action,
590 To prove his cause; he'll give full satisfaction
At sword's point; order that, and he'll obey.
Till then, I'll answer for him, come who may.

DON FERNAND

You lack respect; but you are young in age
And I'll forgive the ardor that can rage
595 In a young heart. A king, with wiser goals,
Is more protective of his subjects' souls:
I watch out for my own, my cares preserve
Their lives: the head must guard the limbs that serve
The body. Thus, what may seem right to you
600 Does not to me: you speak as soldiers do,
While I must act as king. In spite of all
You or the Count may think, he cannot fall
From honor by obeying me. This case,
Moreover, touches *me*. To thus disgrace
605 The tutor of my choice is to mock *me*,
And challenge my supreme authority.
No more on that. Besides, ten vessels bearing
Our old foes' colors have been sighted, daring
To reach the river mouth and anchor there.

DON ARIAS

610 Numerous defeats have made the Moors aware
Of your great might; I'm sure they dare no more
To face so great and strong a conqueror.

DON FERNAND

They never, I'm afraid, will learn to see
Andalusia without jealousy
615 While we rule this fine land, which was once theirs,
In spite of them; this great jealousy dares
Their pride, and this is why ten years ago
I made Seville our capital: to know
Just how to foil their plans and to command
620 Prompt action, seeing them as closer hand.

DON ARIAS

Their leaders killed by you, they know, I'm sure,
Your presence makes your conquests quite secure.
You have nothing to fear.

DON FERNAND

                                        Nor to neglect:
Such overconfidence has the effect
625 Of courting danger. Think of just how near
They are, how the high tide could bring them here
So easily. Still, I'd be wrong, at such
Uncertain news, to go and cast too much
Panic in people's hearts: a useless fright
630 Would sweep the city and alarm the night.
Double the watches on the walls instead.
Enough for tonight.
                          (Exit Don Arias)

Le Cid

Scene 7——DON FERNAND, DON SANCHE, DON ALONSE

(Enter Don Alonse)

DON ALONSE

Sir, the Count is dead:
Through his son's hand, Don Diegue has been avenged.

DON FERNAND

I knew Rodrigue would seek to be revenged,
635 But hoped to avert this tragic happening.

DON ALONSE

Chimene, demanding justice, comes to bring
Her sorrow to your feet—she's all in tears.

DON FERNAND

I sympathize with her; yet, it appears
To me the Count deserved full worthily
640 This punishment for his temerity.
His death may have been justified—and yet
I can't lose such a man without regret.
After a lifetime's service to the State,
And all the blood he's shed for me, his fate
645 Cannot but grieve me and shake the Crown; despite
His pride, I feel his loss and miss his might.

SCENE 8——DON FERNAND, DON DIEGUE, CHIMENE, DON SANCHE,
DON ARIAS, DON ALONSE
(Enter Don Diegue, Don Arias, Chimene)

CHIMENE

Justice, Sir, justice!

DON DIEGUE

Ah, Sir, hear us, please.

CHIMENE

I fall at your feet.

DON DIEGUE

I embrace your knees.

CHIMENE

I ask for justice, Sir.

DON DIEGUE

Hear my defense.

CHIMENE

650   Punish this youth's audacious insolence.
He has destroyed the safeguard of your throne,
Has killed my father.

DON DIEGUE

And avenged his own.

CHIMENE

A king must act when subjects' blood is spent.

DON DIEGUE

A just revenge deserves no punishment.

DON FERNAND

655   Rise, both of you, and speak at ease. Chimene,
       I share your grief and I do feel your pain:
       An equal sorrow also touches me.
(*To Don Diegue*) You turn will come, don't interrupt her plea.

CHIMENE

       My father's dead. I saw him when he died,
660   His blood, Sir, streaming from his noble side—
       That blood, which has so often saved this town,
       That blood, which has won battles for the Crown,
       That angry blood, which smoked in glowering
       At being shed for others than its King,
665   Which danger dared not shed, knowing its worth—
       Rodrigue has, in your court, spilled on the earth.
       I ran out, weak and pale, to that dread spot
       And found my father lifeless—I cannot
       Continue, Sir, my voice begins to fail;
670   My grief-filled tears and sighs must end this tale.

DON FERNAND

       Courage, my child, and hear what I now say:
       Your king becomes your father as of this day.

CHIMENE

       You grant my misery too much honor, Sir.
       I found him lifeless, as I've said—to stir
675   My soul, his blood gushed from his left side, writing
       My duty in the dust, further inciting
       My heart to seek revenge, speaking to me
       Through wounds, reduced to wordless bravery.
       To plead his case to the most just of kings,
680   Through my sad voice his message he now brings:
           Sir, do not suffer that beneath your might
       Such license reign before your very sight,
       For through this wicked license you expose

Your bravest men to rash temerity's blows,
685   Letting an upstart youth destroy their glories,
Bathe in their blood, and mock their famed life-stories.
If such brave warriors die this way, without
Revenge, the zeal to serve you will die out.
My father's death demands revengeful action,
690   More for your sake than for my satisfaction.
You lose through such a death: for your own good,
Avenge it with another—blood for blood.
Exact a sacrifice—not to myself,
But to your crown, your kingdom, and yourself;
695   Sacrifice, Sir, for Spain's own good, all they
Who glory in crimes as cruel as this today.

DON FERNAND

Don Diegue, reply.

DON DIEGUE

How enviable is he
Who, when he's lost his strength, can instantly
Lose life! For what sad fates the drawn-out years
700   Bring noble men at close of their careers!
I, whose long labors won such fame for me,
I, followed everywhere by victory,
Now see myself, for having lived too long,
Insulted, vanquished, suffering a great wrong.
705   What neither combat, siege, nor traps could do,
Nor mighty Aragon and Granada too,
Nor all my rivals nor your enemies,
The Count has done, in your own court, with ease,
Under your very eyes, in jealous rage,
710   Proud of his advantage over my age.
Sir, thus these hairs grown grey in armor-blue,
This blood, so often spilled in serving you,
This arm, at one time feared by every foe,
Would have descended to the grave in low
715   Disgrace—save that my son proved worthy of me,
Worthy of Spain, and of your majesty.
He lent me his strong arms, killed in my name,
Restored my honor, washed away my shame.
If showing courage and righteous discontent,

720   If just revenge deserve a punishment,
       On me alone the tempest's blow should fall:
       When the arm sins, the head's to blame for all.
       Whether or not this matter is a crime,
       He's but my arm, Sir—I'm the head this time.
725   Chimene's complaint is that her father's dead;
       Could *I* have killed him, I'd have done it instead.
       So sacrifice the head, this weak old thing,
       But spare the arm which can still serve his king.
       Sir, take my life to satisfy Chimene:
730   I won't resist, I will accept the pain;
       And far from calling it a harsh decree,
       An honorable death satisfies me.

                        DON FERNAND

       This matter is important, calling for
       The full King's Council to discuss it more.
735   Don Sanche, take Chimene home. My Court, your word,
       Shall be your jails, Don Diegue. I have now heard
       You both, and will be just. Go, fetch his son.

                          CHIMENE

       Murderers must die for justice to be done.

                        DON FERNAND

       Go, calm your grief, my child, and take some rest.

                          CHIMENE

740   That merely brings me, Sir, more grief, at best.

ACT 3

Scene 1——DON RODRIGUE, ELVIRE
(Chimene's house)

ELVIRE

You—here! Poor wretch, your madness is too great!

RODRIGUE

I'm following the course of my poor fate.

ELVIRE

What gives you such audacious pride to show
Your face here in the house you've filled with woe?
745 What? would you kill him once again, or face
The poor Count's ghost?

RODRIGUE

                    His life was my disgrace;
My hands accomplished what my honor would.

ELVIRE

But coming to the dead man's house! Why should
A murderer want to seek his refuge there?

RODRIGUE

750 I come to offer up my life, and bear
My body to my judge. Do not look so
Surprised; I seek my death now since I know
I've dealt out death. My judge is my Chimene:
I merit death since I have brought her pain,
755 Deserved her hatred. I'll be glad to stand
Judgment from her lips, death from her hand.

ELVIRE

Flee from her sight, her fury is still hot;
Escape her first transports of grief: do not
Expose yourself to the first volleys I
760   Am sure her feelings will wildly let fly.

RODRIGUE

No, my Chimene cannot show enough wrath
To justly punish me. I choose this path,
For I escape a hundred deaths if I
Can stir her anger, and the sooner die.

ELVIRE

765   Chimene is at the palace, all in tears,
       And will return escorted. Ease my fears,
       Rodrigue: please flee. What would slanderers say
       If someone sees you here? You wish that they
       Add to her misery, accusing her
770   Of harboring her father's murderer?
       She's back! I see her: oh, at least, please hide,
       Rodrigue, for her own honor's sake and pride.

SCENE 2——DON SANCHE, CHIMENE, ELVIRE
(Enter Don Sanche, Chimene)

DON SANCHE

Yes, Madame, blood for blood should avenge your pride.
Your wrath is just, your tears are justified.
775 I don't pretend, by use of words, to try
To calm you nor console you, but if I
Could serve you, do not hesitate to use
My sword to punish him; please don't refuse
My love's offer to avenge this death: your charms
780 And your commands will give strength to my arms.

CHIMENE

Alas!

DON SANCHE

Please do accept—give me your trust.

CHIMENE

I'd wrong the King, who promised to be just.

DON SANCHE

You know how slowly justice works, and crime
Often escapes through much delay and time.
785 The slow, uncertain course of justice can
Cost many tears. Permit a gentleman
To avenge you, then: the way's more swift and sure.

CHIMENE

It is the last resort. When I've no more
Choices, and if your sympathy is still strong,
790 You'll then be free to avenge me of this wrong.

DON SANCHE

That's all my soul desires; since now I know
There's hope for it, contented, I will go.

(Exit Don Sanche)

CHIMENE

At last we are alone, and I am free
To show you how much pain this misery
795   Has brought my soul, give vent to my sad sighs,
Reveal the sorrow that within me lies.
My father's killed, Elvire, by the first sweep
And thrust Rodrigue's sword ever made. Weep, weep,
My eyes, dissolve in tears! One half my life
800   Has sent the other to the grave; this strife
Binds me to avenge the half I've lost, you see,
Upon that half which yet remains to me.

ELVIRE

Compose yourself, Madame.

CHIMENE

                            Ah! What's the good
Of that when misery is so great? How should
805   My sorrow be appeased if I can't hate
The hand that caused the pain? What other fate
Is mine but agony if I pursue
A crime, yet love its perpetrator, too?

ELVIRE

He killed your father, and you love him still!

CHIMENE

810   More than just love: I *adore* Rodrigue, I will
Admit; love and resentment clash in me;
I find my true love in my enemy.
Despite all of my wrath, inside my heart
Rodrigue still fights my father: I feel him start,
815   Attack, yield, and defend himself, now strong,
Now weak, and now triumphant; swept along
By this rough duel of wrath and love, my will

Stands firm, although my heart is torn; thus, still,
Whatever influence love has over me,
820 I shall not hesitate: I clearly see
My duty—I'll follow it implicitly.
Although Rodrigue is very dear to me
And though he owns my heart, yet in my head
I know who I am, and that my father's dead.

ELVIRE

825 You mean to seek revenge?

CHIMENE

                    Alas, cruel thought!
And cruel revenge in whose rough trap I'm caught!
I fear his death, yet want him dead: that *is*
My wish, although *my* death shall follow his!

ELVIRE

No, no, Madame, renounce this tragic plan;
830 Don't force yourself to do what no one can.

CHIMENE

What! in my arms he lay, my father, dying,
And I not heed his blood, which I heard crying
For vengeance! Oh, my heart should then believe
It owes him only powerless tears, deceive
835 Itself, and let a shameful love like this
Stifle my honor in silent cowardice!

ELVIRE

Madame, believe me, you're excused from such
Vengeance against a man you love so much,
Your own true love. You've seen the King, you've done
840 All that you could. Don't force the issue on,
And don't insist on such extreme revenge.

CHIMENE

My honor is at stake, I must avenge
Myself; however much love may beguile,
To noble souls all such excuse seems vile.

ELVIRE

845   You love him, though—he does not displease you.

CHIMENE

It is true.

ELVIRE

Well, then, just what would you do?

CHIMENE

Preserve my honor, end my pains, pursue
My true love to his death, and then die too.

SCENE 4——DON RODRIGUE, CHIMENE, ELVIRE

RODRIGUE

Well, then! No need for more pursuit or strife:
850   You have the honor now to take my life.

CHIMENE

Elvire, where are we? What is it I see?
Rodrigue in my own house, in front of me!

RODRIGUE

Taste, unopposed, the sweetness of my death.
Don't spare my blood—deprive me of my breath.

CHIMENE

855   Alas!

RODRIGUE

Listen to me.

CHIMENE

I die!

RODRIGUE

Chimene—

CHIMENE

Go, let me die.

RODRIGUE

Just a few words, and then
With this sword you can make your vengeance good.

CHIMENE

What! and still dripping with my father's blood!

RODRIGUE

Chimene—

CHIMENE

              Away with the odious thing! The sight
860   Of it recalls your crime, brings it to light.

RODRIGUE

Look at it rather to arouse your hate,
To increase your anger and to speed my fate.

CHIMENE

It's stained with my own blood.

RODRIGUE

                  Plunge it in me,
My blood will wash away yours instantly.

CHIMENE

865   What cruelty to kill a father by
The sword, and then to make his daughter die
With sight of it! Rodrigue, it's I you slay
With it—I can't endure it—take it away!

RODRIGUE

    I will, yet wish your hands would heed my call
870   To end my wretched life once and for all;
For you must not expect me to retract,
Despite my love for you, a righteous act.
The effect of hot-brained anger inalterably
Disgraced my father, brought great shame on me.
875   You know how a slap affects a noble man:
I shared the insult, sought its author, ran

And found him, then avenged my family name.
I'd do it again, if things were still the same.
Not that my love for you did not, in fact,
880   Struggle against my duty in this act.
You judge its power: despite the affronted state
My name stood in, I did deliberate.
Forced to displease you or to stay disgraced,
I still accused myself of too much haste,
885   Of too much violence. And your great beauty
Would certainly have turned me from my duty
If I had not opposed it with this thought:
That a dishonored man deserves you not;
That though I have a place within your heart,
890   If I trade honor for disgrace, you'd start
To hate me; that to heed Love's guileful voice
Makes me unworthy, and defames your choice.
I say it again, and though my heart must sigh
With pain, I will repeat it till I die:
895   I wronged you, but I had to, to preserve
Honor, to efface my shame, and to deserve
Your love. These obligations met, it's you
I now would satisfy. I've come here to
Give up my life. I've done my duty to
900   My father; I do my duty, now, to you.
I know your father's death must turn your love
Against me; I would not deprive you of
Your victim. Sacrifice to his life-blood *me*
Who am proud of having spilled it righteously.

CHIMENE

905   (Ah!) Though you're my foe, Rodrigue, I cannot blame
You for avoiding infamy and shame;
However sorrow makes me cry or groan,
I don't accuse you: I lament my own
Misfortune. After such a blatant action,
910   Honor, I know, demanded satisfaction.
You only did your duty as all fine
Men should; in doing yours, you taught me mine.
You avenged your father and upheld your name:
Your valor shows me I must do the same.
915   I have a father to avenge, like you;
I have my honor to uphold now, too.

Oh! how my love distresses me: if, rather
Than you, another man had killed my father,
My soul would then, in seeing you, receive
920 Its only comfort: *your* charms could relieve
My sorrow, bringing solace if so dear
A hand as yours could wipe away each tear.
Honor, however, demands from me its due:
I've lost my father—and now I must lose you!
925 This dreadful duty's will, tyrannical,
Demands that I myself pursue your fall.
And you must not expect me to retract,
Despite my love for you, this vengeful act.
Though love's persuasive, my nobility
930 Must correspond to yours. By wronging me,
You've proven worthy of me and done your due;
I must, by killing you, prove worthy of you.

RODRIGUE

Defer no more what honor bids you do:
It claims my head; I give it, then, to you.
935 Offer it to this cause: and sweet shall be
The death-blow that your honor awards to me.
To wait for a slow justice would postpone
Your honor, and would just prolong my own
Suffering: I'm happy dying by your hand.

CHIMENE

940 Go, I'm not your executioner, and
Being but the plaintiff, do I have the right
To take your life? I must attack and fight
The life you must defend. To prosecute
Is up to me; others must execute.

RODRIGUE

945 Whatever hold our love has over you,
Your honor must reply to mine; and to
Avenge one's father through another's hand,
Chimene, is no reply, you understand:
My hand alone avenged my father's shame;
950 Your hand alone must avenge your father's name.

CHIMENE

How cruelly you persist! You found revenge
With no one's aid, yet want me to avenge
Myself with yours. I am too noble, too,
To allow my honor to be owed to you.
955   My father and my glory will not share
Their victory with your love or your despair.

RODRIGUE

Harsh point of honor! Ah! whatever I do,
Can I not finally win this boon from you?
In vengeance, or at least in pity, take
960   My life, for your dead father and our love's sake.
Your hapless lover would prefer the fate
Of death at your hand to life with your hate.

CHIMENE

Then go—I hate you not.

RODRIGUE

                          You should.

CHIMENE

                                      I can't.

RODRIGUE

Think of the blame, the gossips who will rant
965   Of this! When they learn you still love me, what
Is there that envy and untruth will not
Dare then to say? Silence them instantly,
And save your own repute by killing me.

CHIMENE

It will, if I spare you, collect more praise;
970   I *want* dark slander's strident voice to raise
My honor to the skies, and mourn my woe,

Knowing I love yet still pursue my foe.
Go—don't confront my sorrow with what I
Must lose and yet still love. Go now, and try
975   To hide your exit in the dark of night;
If people see you leave, my honor might
Court hazard. There will be no need to fear
Slander unless they know that you've been here.
Don't give them means to attack my virtue, too.

RODRIGUE

980   I'd sooner die!

CHIMENE

Go, then.

RODRIGUE

What will you do?

CHIMENE

Though this fine love dispels my wrath, I'll try
My best to avenge my father; yet, though I
Obey such a cruel duty's rigorousness,
My one wish is to be quite powerless.

RODRIGUE

985   O miracle of love!

CHIMENE

O heavy pain!

RODRIGUE

What woes our fathers force on us, Chimene!

CHIMENE

Rodrigue, who would have known—

RODRIGUE

—or thought to say—

CHIMENE

That joy so near could so soon fly away?

RODRIGUE

Or that, so near the port, calm though it seems,
990   A sudden storm would shatter all our dreams?

CHIMENE

O mortal griefs!

RODRIGUE

How vainly we implore!

CHIMENE

Go, I repeat, I will hear you no more.

RODRIGUE

Adieu: I shall mark time, waiting for your
Pursuit to take my life forevermore.

CHIMENE

995   If I succeed, I swear to you that I
Will breathe not one more breath after you die.
Adieu: above all, watch that you're not seen.
        (Exit Rodrigue)

ELVIRE

Madame, however, bad one's luck has been—

CHIMENE

No more, Elvire—please leave me to my moan;
1000   I seek silence and night to weep alone.

SCENE 5———DON DIEGUE
(The public square)

DON DIEGUE *(alone)*

We never taste a perfect happiness,
But find some sorrow inside each success.
Some problems always mar the purity,
In these events, of our felicity.
1005 Amid good fortune I see them appear:
I bathe in joy, and yet I shake in fear.
I've seen the foe who shamed me dead, but I
Can't find the man who cleared my name, and my
Travails are all in vain: a broken man,
1010 I scour the town, the little strength I can
Wring out of my old frame expended on
A fruitless search for this great champion.
Each hour and everywhere in this dark night
I think I can embrace him—but the sight
1015 Becomes a shadow; and my love, misled,
Conceives suspicions filling me with dread.
I find no signs that he has fled; I fear
The dead Count's friends' pursuit; their number here
Frightens me and dismays my mind: my son
1020 Is dead, or else imprisoned, living on.
Just heavens! *Is* it my sole hope I see
At last, or am I still deceived? It's he,
Without a doubt; my wish is granted me,
My fear is gone, my sorrows cease to be.

SCENE 6———DON DIEGUE, DON RODRIGUE

(Enter Rodrigue)

DON DIEGUE

1025   Rodrigue, at last you're here before my eyes!

RODRIGUE

Alas!

DON DIEGUE

Don't spoil my joy with dour sighs;
I'll catch my breath so as to praise you now.
My valor has no cause to disavow
Your own: you've matched it well; the bravery
1030   In you brings back to life the heroes we
Descend from; you are of their stock, through me:
Your first sword-thrust matched all mine brilliantly.
Inspired by a noble drive, your youth
Equaled my fame in this great test. In truth,
1035   You're all my joy, you are an old man's sword;
Touch these white hairs whose honor you've restored;
Come kiss this cheek, and recognize the place
Where fell the affront your valor did efface.

RODRIGUE

I owed it to you: I could do no less,
1040   Being born of you, reared by your watchfulness.
I had good fortune, and I'm glad to know
That my first blow pleased him to whom I owe
My life. But be not vexed if, after you,
I dare to satisfy myself now, too.
1045   Let my despair be free to erupt in force;
Too long have your words blinded it. Of course,
I don't repent the act; but, equally,
Return to me the joy it snatched from me.
For you I fought my heart: this noble blow
1050   Deprived me of my love and brought me woe.
Say nothing more, for I've lost all for you:
I have repaid full well what you were due.

DON DIEGUE

Prize, prize the glory you have gained much more:
I gave you life, in turn you did restore
1055   My pride, dearer to me than life—so much
The more I owe to you. But now from such
A noble heart cast out these weaknesses;
We've but one honor—there are many mistresses!
Love's but a joy—honor's a duty, though.

RODRIGUE

1060   ·What are you saying!

DON DIEGUE

What you ought to know.

RODRIGUE

My injured honor wreaks revenge on me,
And you dare urge me to infidelity!
An equal shame follows the cowardly soldier
And the unfaithful lover both—hold your
1065   Reproof—do not insult my constancy;
Let me be noble without perjury.
My vows won't break so soon—our ties are stronger
Than that; they bind me, though I can no longer
Hope; I can neither leave nor have Chimene:
1070   Death is the sweetest way to end my pain.

DON DIEGUE

It's not yet time to seek your death or meet
Your fate; your country needs your arm; the fleet
We feared is entered on the river, and
Plans to surprise the city and sack the land.
1075   The Moors will come: the tide and night no doubt
Will shortly bring them to our walls without
A sound. The Court's in chaos; all one hears
In town are cries, and all one sees are tears.
In this misfortune, I have chanced to find
1080   Five hundred friends of mine who, of one mind

To avenge me once they heard of my distress,
All came to offer me their services.
You have forestalled them; but their brave hands would,
If dipped in Afric blood, do much more good.
1085   Now honor bids you go stand at their head:
It is by you this brave band would be led.
Go foil the attack of our old enemy:
There, if you wish to die, die valiantly;
Take up this chance, because it's offered you:
1090   Make the King owe his royal safety to
Your death. Rather, return with wreaths upon
Your brow: extend your fame, don't base it on
Just one act; force, by deeds of bravery,
The King to pardon you, Chimene to be
1095   Silenced. The one way to recapture her
And her heart is to come back conqueror.
But time's too dear to waste with words, to be
Talking when you should fly. Come, follow me,
Go fight, and show the King what you can do;
1100   Show him the Count was nothing: he has *you*.

ACT 4

(Chimene's house)

CHIMENE

It's not a false report? You are quite sure?

ELVIRE

Madame, he could not be admired more;
In one great voice his glorious deeds are raised
Up to the sky, and everywhere he's praised.
1105 The Moors appeared—and met shame and defeat;
Their quick attack gave way to quick retreat.
Three hours of combat gave our warriors
Full victory, two royal prisoners.
Their leader's valor met no obstacles.

CHIMENE

1110 And Rodrigue's hand performed these miracles?

ELVIRE

His brave deeds won the two kings that command
The Moors: these two were captured by his hand.

CHIMENE

From whom can you have learned this startling news?

ELVIRE

The crowd sings everywhere his praises, views
1115 Him as their source of joy, joy's messenger,
Their guardian angel, their deliverer.

93

CHIMENE

How does the King view this brave conqueror?

ELVIRE

Rodrigue still does not dare appear before
The King; Don Diegue, pleased, came in Rodrigue's name,
1120 Bringing these royal captives, chained. He came
To ask the bounteous monarch's favor, and
That he deign see the man who saved the land.

CHIMENE

Is Rodrigue wounded?

ELVIRE

           That I do not know.
You turn pale! Don't let your composure go.

CHIMENE

1125 Nor should I let my weakening anger go:
Must I forget myself because I'm so
Concerned for him? He's praised, and I consent!
My honor's mute, my duty impotent!
Be silenced, love; let anger act for you:
1130 Two kings or no, he killed my father, too.
These mourning clothes show my unhappiness:
They were the first results of his prowess
And deeds; though others praise him at this time,
Here everything reminds me of his crime.
1135   You who promote my bitter sentiments—
Veil, crape, dress, and lugubrious ornaments,
Grave pomp brought on by his first victory—
Uphold my honor against my heart, and see
That when my love becomes too strong you speak
1140 To me of my sad duty; don't be weak:
Attack this conquering hero without fear.

ELVIRE

Restrain yourself—the Infante—she is here.

SCENE 2——THE INFANTE, CHIMENE, LEONOR, ELVIRE
(Enter the Infante, Leonor)

THE INFANTE

I come here not to soothe your woes and fears—
Rather, to mingle my sighs with your tears.

CHIMENE

1145 Join in the common joy, instead—be gay;
Taste the good fortune heaven sends your way,
Madame: I only have the right to sigh.
The peril Rodrigue rescued us from by
His deeds, the safety he ensured for us,
1150 Only permit today that I be thus,
In tears. He saved the city, served his king:
Only *I* feel the woe his exploits bring.

THE INFANTE

It's true, Chimene, that he's done wondrous things.

CHIMENE

I've heard this vexing tale. The whole world sings
1155 His deeds, and thus I hear him spoken of:
"As brave in battle as ill-starred in love."

THE INFANTE

What in this public discourse vexes you?
This young Mars whom they praise was able to
Please you, possessed your heart, lived by your voice;
1160 To extol his valor is to praise your choice.

CHIMENE

Everyone can extol it rightfully;
But praise for him brings added pain for me.
It aggravates my grief and agony:
I see how much I lose, seeing what he
1165 Is worth. What cruelty to a lover's soul!

My love for him grows the more men extol
His worth: yet duty's always stronger, and will
Pursue his death, although I love him still.

THE INFANTE

Your duty yesterday placed you in high
1170   Esteem; your effort did so signify
A noble heart, that all in Court admired
Your strength, pitied your love, by duty inspired.
But would you take a faithful friend's advice?

CHIMENE

To disobey your word would be a vice.

THE INFANTE

1175   What was just then's no longer so today,
Chimene: Rodrigue is now our great mainstay,
The people's hope, the man whom they adore,
Castile's defense, the terror of the Moor.
The King himself agrees that, of all men,
1180   In him alone your father lives again;
If you wish me in brief to explain to you—
You seek the country's ruin if you pursue
His death. What! is it ever right to sue
For vengeance when you bare your country to
1185   Its foes? Is action against us justified?
The crime was not ours; why must we be tried
And punished, too? It's not as though you need
Marry the man you must accuse: indeed,
I would myself relieve you of *that* pain;
1190   Deny him your love, but spare us his life, Chimene.

CHIMENE

Ah! it's not up to me to be so kind;
This duty which torments me has, I find,
No limits. Though to him my heart is true,
Though people praise him, and the King does, too,
1195   And though brave men surround him, none the less
I'll crush his laurels beneath my cypresses.

THE INFANTE

It's noble when, so as to avenge your father,
You attack the man you love; but it shows rather
Greater noblesse when one submits blood ties
1200   To public interest. These are no lies,
Believe me. It's enough to quench your love:
You punish him if you deprive him of
Your heart. Let public welfare rule your actions.
Besides, think what will be the King's reactions?

CHIMENE

1205   He may refuse me, but not silence me.

THE INFANTE

My dear Chimene, consider carefully.
I'll leave you now to choose the path you'll take.

CHIMENE

My father's dead—there is no choice to make.

SCENE 3——DON FERNAND, DON DIEGUE, DON ARIAS, DON
RODRIGUE, DON SANCHE
(At the Court)

DON FERNAND

     Brave heir of an illustrious family
1210 That's been the pride and the security
     Of Spain, whose ancestors' great bravery
     Your first essay has equaled, certainly
     My power is too small to reward you,
     To grant you all the merit you are due.
1215 The country freed of its fierce enemy,
     This scepter in my hand upheld for me,
     The Moors defeated ere a call to arms
     Could have been given by me amid these alarms:
     Such deeds don't leave your king the means nor yet
1220 The hope of ever paying back his debt
     To you. But your two captive kings will be
     Your recompense. Both have, in front of me,
     Called you their "Cid," which in their tongue means lord;
     I'll not begrudge this title as your reward.
1225 From now on, be "the Cid": let all who hear
     This name, let every country, quake with fear;
     Let it point out to all *my* subjects, too,
     Your worth to me, and the debt I owe to you.

RODRIGUE

     Sir, let Your Majesty spare me my shame;
1230 So small a service merits not such fame,
     And makes me blush before so great a king,
     For not deserving such distinguishing
     Renown. I know I owe my life-blood and
     My being to the welfare of your land;
1235 And should I lose them for so worthy a cause,
     I'm but a subject, heeding duty's laws.

DON FERNAND

     Not all the subjects who are bound to me
     Discharge their duty with such bravery;
     Brave men must be brave to a fine excess

1240 To serve their kingdom with such rare success.
      So let yourself be praised; and now tell me
      At length the story of your victory.

                    RODRIGUE

      Sir, in this pressing peril of the night
      Which threw the city into such great fright,
1245 I sought my father's house—only to find
      A group of friends who urged my troubled mind . . .
      But, Sir, please pardon my temerity;
      I led them without your authority:
      They were prepared; danger was drawing near;
1250 I risked my head if I had dared appear
      In Court. Since I risked losing my life, too,
      It seemed more sweet to die fighting for you.

                    DON FERNAND

      I pardon you for avenging your offense;
      A rescued nation speaks in your defense:
1255 Henceforth be sure Chimene will speak in vain—
      I'll but console her if she speaks again.
      But go on.

                    RODRIGUE

          Led by me these brave men now
      March out, strong confidence on each man's brow.
      We were five hundred; but we gain support
1260 And are three thousand when we reach the port.
      Seeing us march with such determination,
      Even those most frightened lose their trepidation!
      When we arrive, two-thirds of them I hide
      In holds of vessels lying there beside
1265 The pier; the rest, whose size grows constantly,
      All burning with impatience, stay by me;
      And there we spend, without making a sound,
      A good part of the night, flat on the ground.
      The guards do the same thing by my command,
1270 Hiding themselves to aid the ruse I planned.
      And boldly I pretend to have from you
      The orders which I give to all in view.

The dim light of the stars at last unveils
To sight upon the tide some thirty sails;
1275 The waves form, lifting both the Moors and sea
Up to the harbor jointly. Quietly
We let the Moors pass by; all seems asleep;
No soldiers anywhere in sight; our deep
Silence deceives their minds: how could they doubt
1280 But that they had surprised us? So without
Fear they approach, cast anchor, disembark—
Right in our waiting hands there in the dark.
We then rise up, and, all at once, let fly
A thousand thunderous cries up to the sky.
1285 At this, our men in ships shout their replies,
And come out armed. Confused by all the cries,
The Moors are seized with fear as they alight,
Thinking they've lost ere they've begun to fight.
They came for pillage, only to find war;
1290 We press them hard, both on the sea and shore,
Make their blood run in rivulets before
They can resist or form their ranks once more.
　　　　But soon, in spite of us, they're rallied by
Their kings; courage returns, their fear to die
1295 Dispelled: the shame of death without a fight
Restores their courage, discipline, and might.
They face us firmly and flash their scimitars,
Horribly mingling into their blood ours.
The earth, the fleet, the river and the port
1300 Are fields of carnage, where Death keeps his court.
　　　　(O!) How many deeds, how many a brilliant fight
Go without notice in the dark of night,
Where each man sees but his own mighty blows,
And which way Fate will fall, none of them knows!
1305 I move about, encouraging our men,
Advancing or regrouping them, and when
Others arrive, I lead them to the fray,
Not knowing the outcome till the break of day.
The dawn shows our advantage, finally:
1310 The Moors see they are lost, and suddenly
Lose heart; seeing our reinforcements nigh,
Their will to win cedes to their fear to die.
They reach their ships, and cut the cables, crying
Frightfully up to the sky, while flying
1315 In frenzied haste, without considering

Where their kings are, or what is happening
To them. Their fright's too strong for loyalty:
Brought by the tide, now the ebb takes them to sea,
While yet their kings, and some few of their men,
1320   All wounded by our blows, fight even then,
Selling their lives quite dearly, valiantly.
It is in vain I bid them yield to me:
Scimitars clutched, they choose to ignore my call
At first; but seeing all their soldiers fall
1325   By their feet they concede they've lost the field,
And ask for leaders—I step forth—they yield
To me.
        I sent them both to you; and then
The fight came to an end for want of men
To fight. Thus, in your service, my acts were . . .

SCENE 4——DON FERNAND, DON DIEGUE, DON RODRIGUE, DON
ARIAS, DON ALONSE, DON SANCHE

(Enter Don Alonse)

DON ALONSE

1330   Chimene is here to plead for justice, Sir.

DON FERNAND

Annoying news! Unwelcome obligation!
Go—I won't force on her a confrontation.
To have to send you away is a poor show
Of thanks. Let me embrace you ere you go.
       (Exit Rodrigue)

DON DIEGUE

1335   She'd like to save him, but pursues him still.

DON FERNAND

I've heard she loves him; I shall test her will.
Affect a sadder visage.

SCENE 5——DON FERNAND, DON DIEGUE, DON ARIAS, DON ALONSE,
DON SANCHE, CHIMENE, ELVIRE

(Enter Chimene, Elvire)

DON FERNAND

                Be content
At last, Chimene, you've realized your intent:
Although Rodrigue has overcome our foes,
1340   He died before our eyes, slain by their blows.
Give thanks to heaven for avenging you.
(To Don Diegue)   See how so soon her color changes hue.

DON DIEGUE *(to Don Fernand)*

And see—she swoons—and in this swoon admire,
Sir, the effect of true love's perfect fire.
1345   Her sorrow has betrayed the secrets of
Her soul; you can no longer doubt her love.

CHIMENE

What! Then Rodrigue is dead?

DON FERNAND

                       No, it's not true.
He lives, preserves a constant love for you:
Allay your grief for him, and find relief—

CHIMENE

1350   Sir, one can faint from joy as well as grief:
Excessive joy leaves us devitalized,
And whelms the senses when the soul's surprised.

DON FERNAND

You want us to believe the impossible?
Chimene, your grief was all too visible.

CHIMENE

1355 Well, then! Sir, make it crown my misery,
      And call my swoon the effect of grief; you see,
      It stems from a quite righteous grief: if he
      Should die, his death shall steal his head from me.
      If he's slain in the service of the State,
1360 My vengeance would be lost, my aims and hate
      Betrayed: so fine a death is too unjust
      To me. I ask his death, but yet it must
      Not be a glorious one, not one upon
      The field of honor and high fame, but on
1365 The scaffold; let him die, but for my father,
      Not for Castile—that would not shame him. Rather,
      Death for the State can bring no infamy:
      A noble death brings immortality.
            Thus, I rejoice in Rodrigue's victory:
1370 It liberates the State, and leaves to me
      My victim, noble and renowned, his head
      All crowned with glorious laurel wreaths, instead
      Of flowers—in short, one who's worthy to be
      Sacrificed to my father's memory . . .
1375 Alas! Why indulge in a vain fantasy?
      Rodrigue has nothing now to fear from me:
      Can tears men scorn hurt such an enemy,
      For whom your empire is a sanctuary?
      Under your power, he's left totally free;
1380 As with the Moors, he triumphs over me.
      And justice, choked in their spilled blood, this time
      Is but a trophy to the victor's crime:
      Contempt for justice leaves us following
      His chariot, like another captive king.

DON FERNAND

1385 My dear, these words have too violent a ring.
      To dispense justice, one weighs everything.
      Your father's killed; he was the offender, though;
      And so it's mercy that I now should show.
      Before you attack my clemency, forbear—
1390 Consult your heart: Rodrigue is master there,
      And secretly your love knows thanks is due
      To me, who saves a love like him for you.

CHIMENE

For me! My enemy! Whom I hate, Sir!
My source of woe! My father's murderer!
1395 My just pursuit's not taken seriously:
You think you oblige me by ignoring me.
Since you refuse, Sir, to avenge my woe,
Permit me to resort to arms; my foe
Offended me by arms; by arms alone
1400 I also should avenge myself. Make known
To all your knights I seek his head: whoever
Brings it to me, I shall be his forever.
Sir, let them fight him; and I'll wed the one
Who slays Rodrigue as soon as it is done.
1405 By your authority let this be known.

DON FERNAND

This ancient custom in these parts has grown
Under the guise of punishing a crime,
But just deprives the State, time after time,
Of its best warriors, oft crushing the good
1410 And sanctioning the guilty. So I would
Exempt Rodrigue: he is too dear to expose
To fate's caprice and fortune's fickle blows;
Such a great man's crime, be it what it may,
Is, by the Moors in flight, now borne away.

DON DIEGUE

1415 What! Sir, reverse the laws for him alone,
Laws which the Court's so long observed and known?
What will the people think, or envy say,
If he protects his life, under your sway,
As an excuse not to appear where men
1420 Of honor seek a noble death? For then
Such favors would too much defame his name:
Let him enjoy his victory without shame.
He disciplined the Count, who insulted me:
He was a brave man then, and should still be.

DON FERNAND

1425 Since it's your will, I'll let him fight; but for
Each warrior he defeats, a thousand more
Would come: the prize Chimene named probably
Would make each of my knights his enemy.
To make him face them all is too unfair:
1430 Once in the lists is time enough in there.
    Choose whom you wish, Chimene, choose carefully;
After this duel ask nothing more of me.

DON DIEGUE

Do not excuse those frightened of him from
The field, but leave it open; none will come.
1435 After the fame Rodrigue today has won,
Who's brave or vain enough to take him on?
Who'd risk his life against such an enemy?
Who has such bravery, or temerity?

DON SANCHE

Open the lists, I say: for I am he,
1440 Be it temerity, or bravery.
    Award this boon to my avidity,
Madame: you know what you have promised me.

DON FERNAND

Chimene, you choose him to redress your sorrow?

CHIMENE

I've promised, Sir.

DON FERNAND

Be ready, then, tomorrow.

DON DIEGUE

1445 No, Sir, there is no reason to delay:
He who is brave is ready right away.

DON FERNAND

To leave a battle and fight at once? It's death!

DON DIEGUE

In giving his report he caught his breath.

DON FERNAND

    I bid him rest at least an hour or two.
1450   But lest this duel set other examples, too,
    To prove to all it's with regret I agree
    To a bloody event which never did please me,
    Not I, nor all my Court, shall witness it.
(To Don Arias)   You in the judge's seat alone shall sit:
1455   Make sure that both of them fight honorably,
    And bring the victor, when it's done, to me.
    Whiche'er he be, the same prize shall remain:
    My hand shall then present him to Chimene;
    Her marriage vow shall be, then, his reward.

CHIMENE

1460   (O!) What a harsh law to impose on me, my lord!

DON FERNAND

    Though you complain, your love belies your plaint,
    And would accept Rodrigue without constraint.
    Stop murmuring against such a sweet decree:
    You'll marry him who earns the victory.

ACT 5

SCENE 1——DON RODRIGUE, CHIMENE
(At Chimene's house)

CHIMENE

1465   What! in plain day! Whence such audacity,
Rodrigue? Go, please go; you'll dishonor me.

RODRIGUE

I go to die, Madame, and come to you
Before my death to bid a last adieu.
My heart will not accept, since it is true,
1470   My death, unless I offer it to you.

CHIMENE

You—die!

RODRIGUE

I hasten down that happy path
Which will deliver my life to your wrath.

CHIMENE

You—die! Has Don Sanche then such martial art
As to strike terror in a dauntless heart?
1475   Who makes you now so weak, or him so great?
You've not yet fought, yet think you've met your fate!
He who feared not my father nor the Moor
Despairs to duel Don Sanche, even before
The duel! Your courage, thus, gives way to fright.

RODRIGUE

1480   I hasten to be punished, not to fight;
You seek my death, and my love's constancy

Now takes the will to live away from me.
　　　My courage always is the same, but not
My arm, when it comes to defending what
1485　Displeases you; I'd have found means to die
Last night if I'd fought for myself; but I
Fought for my king, his people, and my land—
I'd have betrayed them if I'd stayed my hand.
My noble soul does not hate life in me
1490　Enough to lose it by such treachery.
Now it concerns *my* interests alone;
You ask my death, I now accept. Your own
Wrath chose another's hand to avenge your woe
(I don't deserve to die by yours, I know):
1495　I'll not resist his blows—more respect's due
From me to anyone who fights for you—
Thrilled that they're dealt by *your* hand, since I know
His sword upholds your honor, I will go
And bare my chest to him, and venerate
1500　Through his hand yours, which sends me to my fate.

CHIMENE

If my sad duty's just severity
Makes me pursue your death in spite of me,
And lays so harsh a law upon your heart
You'll not resist the man who takes my part,
1505　In this blind state remember that, beside
Your life, it's also a matter of your pride:
Whatever fame Rodrigue's name now implies,
He'll be considered vanquished if he dies.
　　　Your honor means much more than I to you
1510　Since it has made you dip your hands into
My father's blood, made you renounce, despite
Your love, your dear hope that someday I might
Be yours: yet now your honor seems so light
You wish to be vanquished without a fight.
1515　What fickleness unmans your strength, and how?
Why did you have it then? Why don't you now?
What? are you noble only to outrage me?
Now you don't have to, where's your bravery?
You'd treat my father with such cruel disdain,
1520　To slay him, and then let yourself be slain?
Don't seek your death, leave that to me, and go:
If not your life, defend your honor, though.

DON RODRIGUE

After your father's and the Moors' defeats,
Why should my glory still need other feats?
1525 It can disdain my own defense and care:
All know my courage and my valor dare
Do anything, and that beneath the sky
Nothing's of greater worth to me than my
Own honor. No, think what you will, but I
1530 Can die without risking my glory, die
Without being charged with loss of courage or
Defeat, without suffering a conqueror.
No, men will only say: "He loved Chimene;
He would not live when he had caused her pain,
1535 Deserved her hate; he yielded to his fate
Which made his mistress seek his death, await
His lifeless head: his noble heart would not
Refuse—for that would be a crime, he thought.
To avenge his honor he denied his heart;
1540 To avenge his mistress he then chose to part
From life, from her, preferring, in this strife,
His honor to Chimene, and her to life."
So thus you'll see that my death in this fight
Won't dim my glory, but make it more bright;
1545 From my glad death this honor will ensue:
That none but I could have contented you.

CHIMENE

Since honor and life won't change your will to die,
Since they are but weak lures, if ever I
Have loved you, dear Rodrigue—return my love
1550 And go defend yourself to free me of
Don Sanche; go fight to save me from a fate
Which would give me to someone whom I hate.
Need I say more? Go and fight valiantly,
To force my hand, to impose silence on me;
1555 If in your heart your love for me still lies,
Then win this duel for which I am the prize.
Adieu: these stray words make me blush with shame.

(Exit Chimene)

RODRIGUE *(alone)*

And *now* what enemy can I not tame?
Though Moor, Navarro, or Castilian,
1560   Come, all whom Spain has raised into brave men,
Unite together in an army, and,
Prepare to fight a love-inspired hand:
Join all your efforts against a hope so sweet;
Your number's still too few to escape defeat.

SCENE 2——THE INFANTE
(The Infante's house)

THE INFANTE *(alone)*

1565   Should I still heed you now, proud royalty,
            Which makes my love a sin?
   Or should I heed Love, whose sweet cogency
   Makes me rebel against this pride within?
            Poor princess, wavering in
1570   This choice—which shall it be?
   Rodrigue, your valor makes you worthy of me;
   Nevertheless, you're still not royalty.

   Pitiless Fate, whose rigors separate
            My glory from my love!
1575   Must the more righteous choice bring me the fate
   Of great unhappiness? O skies above!
            How many torments of
            My heart must I await
   If, always, it can neither uphold my name,
1580   Accept the lover, nor put out love's flame?

   Why scorn so fine a choice? My mind's dismayed
            By my qualms and disdain.
   Though I am meant for one of royal grade,
   Rodrigue, I'll live with pride under your reign.
1585   The two kings in your train
            Have you a monarch made.
   Does not this great name, Cid, which now you gain,
   Show clearly over whom you ought to reign?

   He's worthy of me, but yet he is Chimene's—
1590   My gift brings pain to me.
   No real hate stands between them; love remains;
   They do their duty but regretfully.
            I dare not hope to see
            An end to all my pains,
1595   Since Fate, to punish me, this day decrees
   That love can live between two enemies.

SCENE 3——THE INFANTE, LEONOR

(Enter Leonor)

THE INFANTE

Why are you here, Leonor?

LEONOR

To applaud you for
The peace that you have finally found once more.

THE INFANTE

But I am in turmoil—where is this peace?

LEONOR

1600 "Love thrives on hope, but dies when all hopes cease."*
If so, Rodrigue can charm your heart no more.
You know the duel Chimene's engaged him for:
Since either he must die, or he must wed
Chimene, your soul's healed since your hope is dead.

THE INFANTE

1605 How far from true!

LEONOR

What hope is there to come?

THE INFANTE

Rather, what hope could you prevent me from?
If Rodrigue fights by these conditions, I
Have many cunning schemes to break them by.
Love, this sweet source of my cruel agonies,
1610 Shows many wiles to lovers' faculties.

———————

See line 108.

LEONOR

What could *you* do, if the Count's death could not
Enkindle discord in their hearts, so fraught
With love? For Chimene's conduct clearly shows
It's not from hatred that her vengeance grows.
1615   The duel is granted her, and instantly
She accepts the first man who requests to be
Her champion, shunning all those noble hands
Whose exploits made them famous in these lands.
Don Sanche suffices and deserves the call
1620   Because ere this he's never fought at all:
She likes his lack of all experience;
His lack of fame removes her reticence;
And her complaisance ought to make you see
She seeks a duel that quits her honorably,
1625   That gives Rodrigue an easy victory,
And lets her seem contented finally.

THE INFANTE

I see it well enough, yet I adore,
As rival to Chimene, this conqueror.
What should I do, being so unlucky in love?

LEONOR

1630   You should remember whom you're daughter of:
You love a subject, when you're meant for a king!

THE INFANTE

My love has changed, no longer worshiping
Rodrigue, a simple cavalier, now; no,
No longer does my love regard him so:
1635   I love the man who's done such wondrous things—
The valiant Cid, the master of two kings.
        Yet, I'll give up my love, not to avoid
Blame, but so love like theirs won't be destroyed.
And were he crowned for my sake, still I would
1640   Stand by the gift I made, as well I should.
Since in this duel he's sure to win again,
Let's go once more and give him to Chimene.
And you, who see the arrows in my heart,
Come watch me finish that which I did start.

SCENE 4——CHIMENE, ELVIRE
(Chimene's house)

CHIMENE

1645 How pitifully I suffer now, Elvire!
I can but hope, and I have all to fear.
I have no wish to which I dare consent,
No wish of which I don't quickly repent.
I make two rivals take up arms for me:
1650 The happiest outcome fortune may decree
Shall cost me tears, for both fates do I dread:
My father unavenged; my lover dead.

ELVIRE

Both ways I see you comforted: you'll be
Revenged or you will have Rodrigue; you see,   LOVE VS HONOR
1655 Whatever fate decrees for you, you will
Obtain a spouse and have your honor still.

CHIMENE

What! The object of my hate, or of my wrath!
Rodrigue's slayer or my father's! Either path
Will give to me a husband still besmeared
1660 With blood which to my heart is most endeared,
And either way my soul rebels: I fear
The outcome more than death. Begone from here,
Vengeance and Love, who bring me misery—
At such a price you have no charms for me.
1665 And you, almighty source of my cruel fate,
Without an outcome this duel terminate:
No loser and no victor in this fight.

ELVIRE

That is too harsh an outcome to your plight.
This duel just brings more pain if it leaves you
1670 Compelled to plead for justice, always to
Evince this deep resentment, and pursue,
Always, the death of your true lover, too.
Better that his rare valor crown his brow,
Madame, and force silence on you: allow

1675   The laws of combat to suppress your sighs,
        The King to make you heed your own heart's cries.

                            CHIMENE

        Though he should win, why then accept this fate?
        My duty is too strong, my loss too great;
        Neither the duel nor what the King may say
1680   Will be enough to govern them. He may
        Defeat Don Sanche with very little pain,
        But not quite so the honor of Chimene.
        Despite the King, my honor can, it knows,
        Raise against Rodrigue a thousand other foes.

                            ELVIRE

1685   Take care that in the end Heaven does not
        Punish your pride by avenging you. What!
        You'd still refuse the happy chance to be
        Silenced at last, and silenced honorably?
        What does this duty claim or want? What more?
1690   Or could your lover's death ever restore
        Your father? One bane's not enough to know?
        Must you add loss to loss and woe to woe?
        Go, you do not, with this mad, stubborn view,
        Deserve the lover destined still for you;
1695   And we'll see Heaven strike your lover dead,
        Its just wrath leaving you Don Sanche to wed.

                            CHIMENE

        Elvire, I suffer enough agonies;
        Don't double them with fatal prophecies.
        I would escape them both, if possible;
1700   If not, my hopes are with Rodrigue in full:
        Not that a mad desire makes me thus choose,
        But I'm Don Sanche's if Rodrigue should lose—
        My wish stems from this fear. What do I see,
        Poor wretch? Elvire, I'm done for—woe is me!

SCENE 5———DON SANCHE, CHIMENE, ELVIRE

(Enter Don Sanche)

DON SANCHE

1705   Obliged to bring this sword to where you stood—

CHIMENE

What! and still dripping with my lover's blood?*
Traitor, how dare you face me any more,
Having deprived me of him whom I adore?
　　　Burst forth, my love, now let yourself appear:
1710   My father's avenged, you've nothing left to fear.
The same blow brings my honor surety,
My heart despair, my love its liberty.

DON SANCHE

With calmer spirits hear—

CHIMENE

　　　　　You dare say more,
Base murderer of a hero I adore?
1715   You took him treacherously—one brave as he
Would never have lost to such an enemy.
Go—hope for naught from me, you've served me ill:
Far from avenging me, it's me you kill.

DON SANCHE

What strange idea, which far from hearing my—

CHIMENE *(rushing out)*

1720   You would that I should hear you boast, that I
Should calmly hear you paint so arrogantly
His death, my crime, and your great bravery?

See line 858.

SCENE 6——DON FERNAND, DON DIEGUE, DON ARIAS, DON ALONSE,
DON SANCHE, CHIMENE, ELVIRE
(At the Court)
(Enter Chimene, Elvire, Don Sanche)

CHIMENE

There's no more need, Sir, to conceal from view
What all my efforts could not hide from you.
1725 You know I loved; but to avenge a dead
Father I did demand so dear a head:
Your Majesty itself, Sir, could well see
How love gave way to duty. Finally
Rodrigue is dead, and thus I now can be
1730 His grieving lover, not his enemy.
I owed revenge to him I'm daughter of,
And now I owe these tears to him I love.
Don Sanche has ruined me in my own defense,
And for this I must be his recompense!
1735 If kings be moved by pity, please, my lord,
Revoke a law so harsh; and to reward
Such a cruel victory, all that I own
I leave to him; let him leave me alone;
And in a cloister let me mourn the death
1740 Of father and lover till my dying breath.

DON DIEGUE

At last she loves, my lord, and dares this time
Reveal true love and not call it a crime.

DON FERNAND

Chimene, be not deceived; Rodrigue's not dead;
Don't credit what Don Sanche, the loser, said.

DON SANCHE

1745 Sir, her own passions fooled her in spite of me:
I came to tell her of his victory.
This noble warrior, whom she loves—when he
Disarmed me—said, "Fear not, I'd rather see
The victory left in doubt than see you slain,

1750   Than spill blood which was ventured for Chimene.
      But since my duty bids me see the King,
      You go and tell her of the duel, and bring
      Your sword to her on my behalf." Well, Sir,
      I went—the sword deceived her and made her
1755   Believe I'd won; when she saw me returning,
      She suddenly betrayed her love, burning
      With so much anger and such violence
      I could not win a moment's audience.
           Though beaten, I'm contented, for my part;
1760   Despite the interests of a lover's heart,
      Having lost all, I love my loss no less,
      Since it creates a perfect love's success.

           DON FERNAND *(to Chimene)*

      You need not blush for this fine love, my dear,
      Nor seek the means to disavow it here.
1765   A worthy shame in vain solicits you:
      Your honor's met, your duty is done, too;
      Your father is avenged, for it can be
      Revenge to expose Rodrigue repeatedly
      To danger. Heaven's against it, you can see.
1770   Do something for yourself now, finally,
      And don't rebel against my sweet command
      Which gives to him you love your loving hand.

SCENE 7——DON FERNAND, DON DIEGUE, DON ARIAS, DON
RODRIGUE, DON ALONSE, DON SANCHE, THE INFANTE, CHIMENE,
LEONOR, ELVIRE

(Enter the Infante, Leonor, Rodrigue)

THE INFANTE

Now dry your tears, Chimene; receive from your
Princess's hands this noble conqueror.

RODRIGUE

1775 Don't be offended if, before you, Sir,
My love bids me kneel down in front of her.
    I come not to collect my prize, Chimene,
But to present my head to you again.
Madame: my love for you does not require
1780 The law of combat nor the King's desire.
If all that's done will not yet satisfy
A father, tell me then what I should try.
Must I fight thousands more, my deeds extend
To both ends of the world, storm or defend
1785 A camp alone, rout armies, and exceed
The fame of fabled heroes? If indeed
My crime can be thus washed away, I dare
Do all, and can achieve all, too, I swear;
But if this proud, unbending honor won't
1790 Be satisfied unless I die, then don't
Send mortal might against me any more:
My head lies at your feet: take vengeance, for
Your hands have the sole right to conquer a man
Unconquerable; do what no others can.
1795 But let death be enough to punish me:
Don't banish me from your own memory.
And since my death preserves your honor, you
In turn try to preserve *my* memory, too,
And say sometimes, mourning this life I led,
1800 "But that he loved me, he would not be dead."

CHIMENE

Arise, Rodrigue. Sir, I confess it now,
I've said much more than I could disavow:

Rodrigue has virtues I can't hate. I know
When kings command, I should obey. But though
1805 You have condemned me already, could you stand
The sight of such a marriage? You command
This effort from my duty—but is your
Full justice in accord with it? If for
The State Rodrigue's such a necessity,
1810 Must I for his deeds be the salary,
Soiling eternally my own good name,
My hands dipped in my father's blood and shame?

DON FERNAND

What seems at first inexorable crime
Has oft been made legitimate through time:
1815 Rodrigue has won you; you are his, it's true.
But though today his valor conquered you,
I would needs be your honor's enemy
To give him the prize of his victory
So soon. These delayed nuptials don't vacate
1820 A law which gives you to him, since no date
Was set. You'll have a year to mourn if you
Would like. Rodrigue must take up arms anew,
Meanwhile. Although at home we beat the Moor,
Baffled his plans, pushed back his drive, the war
1825 Must be pursued in his own land:
            (To Rodrigue)   Command
My armies; go, attack, ravage their land.
The mere name Cid will leave them quivering;
They named you lord, and will want you for king.
But amid these deeds remain a faithful lover;
1830 Come back, if possible, still more worthy of her,
That, by your acts, so prized becomes your life,
She can't then but be proud to be your wife.

RODRIGUE

To win Chimene, and serve my sovereign, too,
What can you order that I cannot do?
1835 Though I must bear with being so far from her,
I now can hope, and I am happy, Sir.

DON FERNAND

Hope in your courage, hope in my word, too;
Your love's heart is already won by you;
As to Chimene's continued wavering,
1840 Leave that to time, your valor, and your king.

Backgrounds and Discussion

1

Pierre Corneille: 1606–1684

Chronology

Corneille's plays are listed by approximate first performance (many of the exact dates are disputed).

1606   Pierre Corneille born 6 June in Rouen, son of a bourgeois lawyer.

1615–22   Student in Rouen's fine Jesuit school, where he excels, winning the Latin versification prize in 1618 and 1620.

1624   Admitted to the bar in Rouen; tradition holds that he pleaded only one case in his life.

1625   Thomas Corneille born, who would be greatly influenced by brother Pierre in his own successful career as a dramatist.

1628   Corneille's father buys Pierre two magisterial offices in Rouen, which impress on him a number of continuing official duties for the next two decades.

1629–30   According to tradition, the celebrated actor Montdory and his troupe (of the Marais) pass through Rouen; Corneille submits his first comedy, *Mélite*, to Montdory, and the troupe puts it on in Paris. The play's success helps firmly establish the troupe; Corneille's dramatic career is launched.

1631   *Clitandre*, tragicomedy.

1632   *Mélanges poétiques*, volume of verse.
       La Veuve, comedy.

1633   *La Galerie du Palais*, comedy.

1634   *La Suivante*, comedy.
       La Place Royale, comedy.

1635   *Médée*, Corneille's first attempt at tragedy.

The "Five Authors" (Corneille, along with Boisrobert, Colletet, L'Estoile, and Rotrou) are founded under the patronage of Cardinal Richelieu, and collaborate on *La Comédie des Tuileries* (of which the third act is probably Corneille's).

1636   *L'Illusion comique,* comedy.

December 1636 or January 1637: *Le Cid,* tragicomedy.

1637   The *Querelle du Cid* ("Quarrel of *Le Cid*"), including Corneille's *Excuse à Ariste,* Scudéry's *Observations sur le Cid,* and the Académie française's *Sentiments de l'Académie sur le Cid.* (See also Chapter 5 of this study.)
            Corneille's father is ennobled. Corneille collaborates (first act) with the "Five" in *L'Aveugle de Smyrne.*

1639   Corneille's father dies.

1640   *Horace,* tragedy.

1641   *Cinna,* tragedy.
            Corneille marries Marie Lampérière, also from the bourgeoisie; they will have six children.

1642   *Polyeucte,* tragedy.

1643   *La Mort de Pompée,* tragedy.
            Le Menteur, comedy.

1644   *La Suite du Menteur,* comedy.
            The first edition (several to follow) of Corneille's collected works published.
            The Academy rejects his candidacy because Corneille doesn't live in Paris.

1645   *Rodogune,* tragedy.

1646   *Théodore, vierge et martyre,* tragedy.
            Corneille again rejected by the Academy; same reasons.

1647   *Héraclius,* tragedy.
            Promising to move to Paris, Corneille is finally elected to the Academy.

1650   *Don Sanche d'Aragon,* heroic comedy.
            Andromède, tragedy.

1651   *Nicomède,* tragedy.
            Pertharite, tragedy.
            Corneille retires from the stage.

1652–56   Corneille publishes his immensely successful verse translation of *L'Imitation de Jésus-Christ.*

1656   Brother Thomas Corneille's greatest stage success, *Timocrate.*

1659   Corneille returns to the stage with *Œdipe,* tragedy.

1660   Publication of the Complete (seventh) Edition of the works, including the three *Discours sur le poème dramatique* and the *Examens* of each play.

1661 *La Toison d'or*, tragedy, in honor of Louis XIV's marriage.

1662 *Sertorius*, tragedy.
Corneille receives a (largely symbolic) annual pension from the King.
Corneille moves from Rouen to Paris.

1663 *Sophonisbe*, tragedy.

1664 *Othon*, tragedy.

1666 *Agésilas*, tragedy.

1667 *Attila*, tragedy; performed by Molière's company.

1670 *Tite et Bérénice*, heroic comedy.
L'Office de la Sainte Vierge, translation.

1671 *Psyché*, a balletic comedy written jointly by Corneille, Molière, Quinault, and Lully.

1672 *Les Victoires du Roi en Hollande*, poem.
Pulchérie, heroic comedy.

1674 *Suréna*, tragedy.
Corneille's pension is revoked for no clear reason, and is not reinstated until 1682.

1676 The King has six of Corneille's tragedies produced at Versailles.

1680 Corneille's translations of *Les Hymnes de saint Victor* published.

1682 Complete Edition of Corneille's Theatrical Works.

1684 Corneille dies, 1 October, in Paris.
His brother replaces him in the Academy.

Born in Rouen in 1606 and dead in Paris in 1684, Pierre Corneille enjoyed a long and distinguished literary career that included thirty-two plays and a number of poetic works. A great tragic poet and playwright, he was the dominant force in the French stage for much of the seventeenth century and was, along with Racine and Molière, one of the three leading figures of *le théâtre classique*, that brightest jewel in the rich cultural crown of *le grand siècle* (the great century), that most quintessential French genre in France's literary heyday. Among Corneille's dramatic successes are four masterpieces of the French literary canon: *Le Cid* (enduringly his most popular play), *Horace, Cinna*, and *Polyeucte*. All four (and sometimes also *Rodogune* and *Nicomède*) are traditional French school texts, and well-known adages from *Le Cid* have (like their Shakespearean counterparts in English) entered the parlance of every French schoolboy and girl.

And yet, in spite of Corneille's fame and longevity, we know fairly little about his life. As a young man from an upper middle-class family in Rouen, he followed the family tradition and became a lawyer, and would serve in various official and ministerial capacities for much of his life. In fact, Corneille's life presents a certain paradox, or duality at the least. Unlike Shakespeare, who left Stratford for London during his dramatic career, Corneille wrote most of his plays in Rouen, discharging his magisterial duties, raising a large family, and occasionally coming to Paris to supervise the presentation of his plays: this was Corneille the good family man leading the uneventful life of the provincial bourgeois—a man (schooled by the Jesuits) of straight habits and of simple tastes, ill at ease in the "precious" salons of Paris. But this drab exterior masked a literary genius who not only expressed the heroic ideal and passions of the age, but was in spirit very much like one of his own heroes, steeped in his own sense of fame and *gloire:* a proud literary lion, confident of his place in poetic and dramatic history, but at times arrogant and oversensitive, bickering with rivals and defending his high station among the literary luminaries of his day.

Corneille's career was full of choices. First he chose to study law despite his schoolboy prizes for Latin versification and his composition of numerous poems (some of which were published in 1632 as *Mélanges poétiques*). And once his literary career was launched (with *Mélite* in 1629), he had to choose between poetry and drama, and then between comedy and tragedy. He had his greatest success, *Le Cid,* in 1637, when he was but thirty years old. The earlier works were largely comedies, but his greatest works were all in the tragic mode, between 1637 and 1651—during the late Richelieu and the early Mazarin years, and before the Fronde, the series of political revolts the suppression of which finally destroyed the power of the nobles and confirmed the absolute monarchy. Both the earlier and later works, whether comedy or tragedy, were inferior (although often successful on the stage) to those of this central period, from *Le Cid* in 1637 to *Nicomède* in 1651.

In the early seventeenth century, because the Hôtel de Bourgogne had a virtual monopoly as a permanent theatre in Paris, many of the best acting companies were troupes that traveled through the provinces. One such group, headed by a well-known actor named Montdory, passed through Rouen in the summer of 1629. Corneille, twenty-three years old, showed the actor a draft of his first play; Montdory took it with him to Paris and staged it. *Mélite*'s triumphant success launched Corneille on his dramatic career, and helped establish Montdory's troupe (eventually known as the Marais, the section of Paris where they would be situated) as one of France's two leading companies, second only to the Bourgogne. Like Shakespeare with the Globe, Corneille wrote most of his plays specifically for Montdory and the actors of the Marais, a fact which was probably the greatest single influence in the composition of the plays and the creation/distribution of their dramatis personae.

Before *Le Cid*, the first great work of the Classical Period, Corneille was just one of a group of respected dramatists that included Mairet, Tristan, Rotrou, Scudéry, and others; he was not yet *le grand Corneille*, as he would later be known. But in 1637 the phenomenal success and popularity of his eighth play, a tragicomedy called *Le Cid*, proved clearly his superiority and made his name a household word; all of Paris was enchanted by the play, everyone quoting favorite lines; a popular expression of the time was to say about something praiseworthy that *"Cela est beau comme 'le Cid' "* ("That is lovely, like *The Cid*"). Corneille was suddenly France's leading dramatist. Scudéry and Mairet, at once jealous of Corneille's triumph and provoked by his own undisguised self-satisfaction, began a literary war of pamphlets, denigrating both the play and its author. Corneille and his supporters responded in kind, and many of the leading literary figures participated in this poisonous exchange of pamphlets which has become known as the *Querelle du Cid* (the Quarrel of *Le Cid*). The debate grew to such scandalous and venomous proportions that Richelieu finally intervened by silencing both sides and referring the issue to the newly founded Académie française for judgment. The findings of the Académie, carrying Richelieu's stamp of approval but largely written by Chapelain, form a document of startlingly petty pedantry, critical of *Le Cid* by quibbling over minutiae and petty rules about the tragic stage, in spite of the obviously compelling quality of the drama itself, which had so moved the theatregoing audience. But the result of the Querelle would shape the course of French literary and aesthetic values, as well as define the parameters of the continuing polemic between *les doctes* and *les ignorants*, the scholars and the public; it was the most important literary controversy of the century, and I have devoted a separate section to the Quarrel of *Le Cid* (in Chapter 5).

The Academy's unfavorable verdict may have discouraged Corneille and inhibited his creative production temporarily, for after *Le Cid* there was a silence of three years. But such longstanding speculations must be balanced by the fact that Corneille then unveiled his three greatest tragedies in quick succession: *Horace*, a study of patriotism, friendship, and love, in 1640; *Cinna*, a drama involving human mercy and the politics of State, in 1641; and *Polyeucte*, a Christian tragedy of love (both human and divine) and martyrdom, in 1642. But Corneille had learned his lesson: the three tragedies maintained the unities and the dramatic rules so well and strictly that they were to shape the essential guidelines for the definitive form of the French classical tragedy, the genre par excellence of seventeenth-century France.

The rest of that decade found Corneille busily involved both with family life (he married in 1641) and with trying out new and different forms of tragedy. Richelieu's death in 1642 left Corneille temporarily without patronage, but Richelieu's successor Mazarin soon renewed Corneille's pension, although Mazarin had not himself the literary interests of his predecessor. This period of Corneille's dramatic writing culminated in the 1651 production of *Nicomède,* a very Cornelian tragic drama extolling the power and triumph of will in a noble hero surrounded by a world of baseness and intrigue.

After the dismal failure of *Pertharite* in 1651–52, however, Corneille, perhaps feeling that his time was past, announced his retirement from the stage; he wrote no plays for six or seven years. Scholars have in their various speculations perhaps overstated the causes for this second hiatus of silence, for Corneille was hardly inactive during these years. He continued to revise his plays for the several editions of the complete works; he began writing the three *Discours* and the *Examens* (of each play) which would be printed in the 1660 edition and in which he argued and defended his critical theories and practices as a playwright. Most of all, he worked on the *Imitation de Jésus-Christ,* a religious poem (in translation of a fifteenth-century Latin devotional tract, probably by Thomas a Kempis) of over 13,000 lines; it came out in several editions, published between 1651 and 1656; these were highly successful, both popular with the reading audience and lucrative for Corneille.

In 1659 Corneille returned to the stage with *Œdipe;* but his plays henceforward met with mixed success, and occasionally dismal failure. In 1661, Mazarin died and Louis XIV, announcing that *"L'état c'est moi"* ("The State is I"), consolidated the absolute monarchy established by Richelieu and Mazarin and confirmed by the Fronde in 1653. With the passing of the age of Louis XIII and with the accompanying development around Louis XIV of a new set of aesthetic sensitivities (which eschewed formal tragedy for comedy, farce, and pageantry), the age and spirit Corneille knew so well was coming to an end, and his creativity never regained its earlier vigor. Although both he and Racine continued their respectful but intense rivalry for the tragic stage (as well as for the love of Mademoiselle Du Parc, the leading actress of Molière's troupe), they were both being eclipsed by the younger Molière and his more current talents on the comic stage. Corneille continued until 1674 *(Suréna)* to try to regain his former *gloire,* but the age that had idealized and understood the larger-than-life Cornelian hero with noble passions and pride of self was no more.

2

The Political and Social Milieu

To the French, the seventeenth century is *le grand siècle*, and Louis XIV, who reigned for much of the century (1643–1715), was *le grand monarque, le roi soleil* (the Sun King). For this was a period not only of material and continental grandeur, but of literary flowering: this was the French classical period, as central to French literary history as Shakespeare's age is to the English tradition. But while the French have always embraced Shakespeare, the French classical drama—so much the essence of France in the seventeenth century—has always seemed foreign in both spirit and form to the Anglo-Saxon mentality. Thus it is important to have some clear notions about the age and the milieu which spawned such great works as *Le Cid* (1637), *Phèdre*, and *Le Misanthrope*.

The central fact of seventeenth-century French sociopolitical history was the establishment of the absolute monarchy. By the time Louis XIV began his personal rule in 1661 (after Mazarin's death), the absolute monarchy was a *fait accompli*. The preceding sixty years led up to this state of affairs through various struggles between the royal powers and the insubordinate nobles, *les grands* (The Great Ones), as they were called. It was in such an atmosphere that Corneille wrote all his major works.

When Henri IV died in 1610, leaving Louis XIII to be a child ruler, *les grands* hoped to restore France into a semifeudal oligarchy; they denounced the regency of the Queen Mother, Marie de Médicis, and began new uprisings in the hope of returning the centralized royal power to the lords. Marie, however, appointed Cardinal Richelieu her adviser, and this extraordinary man first defeated the rebellious Protestants (in alliance with the English) at La Rochelle in 1629, and then broke the power base of the nobles by destroying their strongholds and by relieving them of the duties of provincial administration—duties he entrusted instead to bourgeois bureaucrats

131

whom he appointed and who were responsible only to him. Even after Louis XIII reached his majority, the young king found Richelieu too useful to dispense with, and between 1624 and 1642, when the Cardinal died, Richelieu was the nation's prime minister, ruling with virtually unlimited authority.

Although Richelieu was of noble origin himself, he fought against the continuing intrigues and rebellions of the Great Ones because he believed in the absolute monarchy and the need to strengthen the power of France; the nobles, conversely, adhered to the heroically independent warrior spirit of feudal times, loath to recognize a centralized authority, even in internal affairs. "Here was the reason," writes André Maurois, "for the harsh edicts against duelling [most familiar to English audiences through Alexandre Dumas's *The Three Musketeers*], which Richelieu punished with death, and it was at this time that the aristocracy 'turned to gallantry because it could no longer turn to tragedy.' "[1] Realizing that France needed internal unity in order to achieve security abroad, Richelieu was intolerant of any sort of dissidence, establishing strict regulations over the nobility, and securing absolute power for himself and the king. In 1636, the Spaniards (in alliance with Austria) invaded France, reaching Corbie. "The country supplied soldiers and money. It was the year of the first production of *Le Cid* [ironically about medieval Spain], and noble feelings inspired noble exploits. Spain was repulsed."[2] A series of foreign victories followed. *Le Cid* itself is a story set, as Robert J. Nelson points out, in "a royal court threatened from within by unruly barons and from without by ancient enemies."[3] Richelieu died in 1642, but by then he had managed to establish, through his absolute power and strict regulations, the triumph of nationalism and French greatness abroad. It was an achievement he sought even in the literary field, where his patronage, encouragement, and direct involvement in literary matters allowed for the flowering of the classical period. As Maurois writes: "When in 1635 he founded the French Academy, he wanted even the Republic of Letters to recognize his authority—and it was a most reasonable authority— over language and the works of the mind. Someone said of him that he had been 'the schoolmaster of the French nation.' "[4]

Within months of Richelieu's death in 1642, Louis XIII died, too; Louis XIV was only five years old. Relieved to be free of the yoke of Richelieu, the nobles approved the regency of the Queen Mother, Anne of Austria—who then surprised them all by appointing one of Richelieu's aides, Cardinal Mazarin, to play much the same role as Richelieu had played. (A popular saying of the time maintained that "the queen hated work but loved Mazarin.") Mazarin continued the business of solidifying French nationalism. Angered by the continuation of absolutism under a woman and an Italian (and, most bitter of all, a bourgeois—at least Richelieu had been an aristocrat), the factious lords staged a succession of uprisings between 1648 and 1653—a preview of 1789, but with vastly different results—collectively known as *La Fronde*. But the erratic and backstabbing behavior of these self-serving *grands* was such that the rebellious nobles not only ensured their own failure but lost all popular support, having reduced the French aristocracy to an international laughingstock. Instead of achieving independence from absolute rule, the Fronde discredited freedom, leaving the aristocracy in a state of humiliation and servility from which it would never quite recover.

Mazarin continued Richelieu's nationalist policies, strengthening French influence abroad, reducing greatly the rival Austrian power. The Peace of Westphalia ordered European affairs in a manner advantageous to France; the Peace of the Pyrenees in 1659 relegated Spain to a subordinate role. When Mazarin died in 1661, the absolute monarchy was secure. When Louis XIV, choosing now to reign alone, boasted that he was the State *(L'état c'est moi),* "he was merely consecrating a situation that had been realized in 1653."[5] The long and glorious rule of *le roi soleil* had begun.

It was during this period that Corneille wrote all his great plays, which often mirror undercurrents of external events. *Le Cid* particularly reflects the life under Richelieu. It is the most exemplary statement of the chivalric-courtly ideals of its day, coming into conflict with the authority of the absolute monarchy.

In the previous century and in the first thirty years of the seventeenth, the French nobility was still relatively rude, ignorant, and unrefined, espousing the old warrior values of the feudal tradition—in *Le Cid*, they would be represented by the older generation, Rodrigue's and Chimène's fathers. The drama of the period was equally unsubtle, based on action, violence, or farce. But there was a growing, cultured and educated noble class, concerned with manners and social refinement, which, during the Richelieu years (1624–42) came into prominence with the stable and centralized royal court in Paris and was complemented by the cardinal's own cultural/intellectual interest and patronage: in 1610, the young marquise de Rambouillet, disgusted by the vulgarity of the court and its nobles, had started a salon for her friends, cultivating good manners, language, spirit, and delicacy of sentiments. The celebrated Hôtel de Rambouillet became France's first "salon"; others soon followed, and these centers of culture and manners raised the French sophistication and reputation for *politesse* to such a level that France became known as the international center of gentility and polish. The salon ladies having been called *les précieuses* (the precious ones), this movement toward refinement became known as *préciosité* (preciousness). By Molière's time preciousness, deprived by the monarchy of the fierce warrior spirit implicit in independent feudal states and the chivalric dueling code, had lost its heroic aspects and had degenerated into the kind of courtly and affected foppishness that Molière so loved to satirize. But during the Richelieu years the combination of preciousness with the hardy warrior spirit produced an elevated chivalric-heroic-courtly code of values and behavior, governing both honor and love, which became the fervent ideal of the age. As Robert Brasillach and other modern critics have shown, "The Cornelian interpretation of reason, honor, love, and the struggle between duty and passion were all typical elements of the period and Corneille did not create new ideas but translated [them]."[6] Further, as Paul Bénichou notes, the romances of *précieuse* literature are "full of heroic or magnanimous sentiments and acts, and Cornelian grandeur of soul is constantly linked there with tenderness in keeping with the conventions of chivalric literature. . . . Ideal love, the courtly tradition, and the spirit of the romances are not different, and are found together in Corneille."[7]

One major reason that succeeding generations (and foreigners) have frequently undervalued and misinterpreted Corneille is their inability to see Cornelian drama as anything else than the advocacy of either the human will or personal honor; they did not understand that his contemporary audience admired his heroes—especially the Cid—for their romantic élan, ardor, and ability to move and ignite the emotions. As Bénichou notes, "Passion in Corneille was entirely steeped in the atmosphere of aristocratic pride, glory, nobility, and romance that pervaded France during the reign of Louis XIII, and permeated the entire literature of that epoch. Under Louis XIV, the sublime as Corneille had envisioned it already seemed a bit archaic."[8] No longer able to share in the *grandes passions* of Corneille's *grandes âmes* (great souls), the following generations interpreted the elevated sublimity and passions of Corneille's heroes as the cold rationalizations of the intellectual will or as straitjacketed morality. "Thus in Corneille's own century, he is at one point praised to the skies for his power to ignite emotions, and at another denied both heat and passion."[9]

The inspiration behind Cornelian theatre—sublime in its lofty tone, full of hubristic heroes, glorifying both pride and love—was largely feudal, combining the bravado of the warrior-barons and the courtly love ideals of the chivalric age. These medieval values blossomed once more in the years prior to *Le Cid*, "when favorable conditions, the renewed prestige of the nobility, and political unrest created the conditions for their most dazzling development. . . . [A] certain kind of passion, inseparable from the aristocratic tradition, inspires all of [Corneille's] heroes."[10] The Cid is a seventeenth-century spiritual descendant of Lohengrin and the Chevalier Bayard.

Corneille, in writing *Le Cid*, was brilliantly able to adapt a story about eleventh-century Spain to the heroic ideals of his own age in seventeenth-century France. In a period when the *hôtel de Rambouillet* shone in its full glory, Corneille illustrated in his play all the great passions of the romanesque ideal developed in the salons: the larger-than-life capacity for romantic love in Rodrigue and Chimène, based on their equally grand sense of self-esteem and generosity of spirit. There could not have been two lovers better conceived to entrance the audiences of an age enchanged by the romance and the baroque. The discipline of classical tragedy would come later—this was the world of tragicomedy and the romanesque, a society that admired *la générosité* of feelings to a fine excess: pride, audacity, adventure, action, romantic love. While Rodrigue may be a descendant of the chivalric heroes of medieval *ballades,* he also represents the sublime ideals most admired in the courtly life under Richelieu: the fearless cultivation of both love and ambition in an adventurous environment fraught with unsought-for-dangers.[11]

Great pride in oneself and one's rank, demanding an equally high level of sentiment and behavior—such pride, which in Christian values was clearly sinful, was the greatest virtue and the source of all great passions in chivalric values. Implicit in such a set of values is the concept that heroism is not subject to a universal law or to Reason, but rather that it strives to attain its own ideals, to fulfill the self, to achieve perfect love, and to attain free will. In order to understand such heroism, we must discard the nineteenth-century concept of a moral Law to which the will and personal passions must submit; as Antoine Adam writes: "Cornelian heroism corresponds to an epoch in our [French] history when personal energy was, on the contrary, considered the highest of values" (my translation).[12]

Martin Turnell points out, in comparing the English and French literatures of the seventeenth century, that "English poetry retained its native vigour, and the primitive folk-element which was present in all medieval art, until the latter part of the century; but in France poetry became more and more the expression of a civilized *élite.* The emphasis falls on decorum, on the virtues of clarity and order, and there is a growing horror among French writers of 'Gothic barbarism.' "[13] In an age of decorum and authority, the password used most frequently is *les règles*—the rules, whether in government, religion, personal behavior, or literature. "There [was] an immense effort," Daniel Mornet wrote in his *Histoire de la littérature et de la pensée françaises,* "to establish everywhere an order which [was] reasonable as the order of mathematics, to organize a sort of social and aesthetic geometry."[14] As with the later neoclassical age (Pope, Swift, et al.) of eighteenth-century England, "the whole tendency of the century was to express itself in brief, pithy maxims. . . . The literary forms chosen by poets and prose-writers—the alexandrine, the maxim and the character—were used both as an intellectual discipline and to present complex material in the most lucid and orderly manner possible."[15] The alexandrine couplet, with its symmetrical balancing of line to line, rhyme to rhyme, or even half-line (with medial *césure*) to half-line—was especially well-suited to such neat and orderly epigrams, proverbs, or repartees. *Le Cid* is full of such ordered and quotable quotations, committed to the collective memory of generations of Frenchmen: *Mais qui peut vivre infâme est indigne du jour* (line 284: "But live in shame and you deserve to die"); *Ma plus douce espérance est de perdre l'espoir* (135: "My greatest hope is but to hope no more"); *Et lorsque le malade aime sa maladie, / Qu'il a peine à souffrir que l'on y remédie* (525–26: ". . . When sick men love their maladies, / They suffer most when they find remedies"). One could cite many more well-known Cornelian maxims. Obviously the age reflected a confidence in the basic reasonableness, order, and sanity of the universe.

Where did such a mania for order originate? In the sixteenth century France had been badly shaken by the religious wars between Catholics and Protestants; as Richelieu and the young Louis XIII took over, there was great uncertainty about the nation's internal future (the aristocracy's desire to return to feudal states) as well as external future (war with Spain and threats from other nations). In retrospect, we can see in the century a strong desire and striving for order and sanity, which was finally imposed on the nation from above, by Richelieu and the absolute monarchy.[16] In this sense, Corneille's and Racine's plays mirrored the contemporary history of ideas.

But in Corneille, as in the early Classical Period in which he wrote—when Richelieu was still striving to establish the absolute monarchy—there is always a tension, a balance between the order and authority of his form and the implicit insurgency of his content. Many of his plays open with a shock, an eruption which threatens established order, reason, or authority: a prohibited duel in *Le Cid;* a bloody feud between families joined by marriage in *Horace;* a political conspiracy in *Cinna;* a religious conversion in *Polyeucte.* *Le Cid,* in fact, may be interpreted (and has been, primarily by Bénichou) as an antiroyalist play, a nostalgic but mildly inflammatory exercise which found favor with its aristocratic audience because it recounts the good old days, when the monarchy was less severe and absolute, and when the nobles could settle their own affairs by themselves through duels, prowess in battle, and the old traditions—with a sympathetic king looking on, but helpless to interfere.

This was not the monarchy Richelieu wanted for his protégé, however, and this old tradition of independent nobles and feuding warriors he was of course determined to stop; the celebrated prohibition on dueling was only the most visible manifestation of his attempt to order and regulate French life at every level and in every respect. Another such manifestation was the increasing regulation of literary works, exemplified by the founding of the Académie française. While Richelieu's interest in literature and his patronage/encouragement (including his creation of the "Five Authors" collaborative group, of which Corneille was a part) helped give the classical drama its impetus, the growing regulation (*les règles,* the rules) of the nature of classical tragedy was partly a taste imposed on authors like Corneille (in which the "Quarrel of *Le Cid*" had a major role) by academics and critics who influenced Richelieu and the Academy—especially Jean Chapelain and later the abbé d'Aubignac. Chapelain headed the Academy, with Richelieu's backing.

A number of academics and literati had been for years in the habit of meeting regularly for discussions and readings. Richelieu invited them to "become a body and assemble under a public charge" (my translation),[17] and thus in 1635 the French Academy was founded. Its membership limit of forty has remained constant to this day. A unique institution, it has held the charge over the centuries of being the arbiter of the French language and of acceptable literary tastes. One of its earliest tasks was the creation of a dictionary of *bon usage*, a guide to proper literary language. This was a collection of words and expressions used by the best writers and by good society *(la bonne société);* all archaisms, technical terms, vulgarities, and material references were excluded. Finally completed in 1694, the dictionary remains a testament both to the sublime language of the great classical period and to its spirit of absolutism and regulation.

As Bénichou suggests, "The spirit of absolute monarchy tended to impose a certain orderliness in all spheres of life,"[18] including the regulation of both love and honor by societal norms and by royal edict. We see this in *Le Cid* in the choices by Rodrigue and Chimène to follow the social priority of familial honor in spite of their love for each other; in the King's attempt to regulate the *affaires d'honneur* among his feuding nobles; and in the King's edict that Chimène must wed the victor of the duel between Rodrigue and Don Sanche.

How is one to judge a dramatic genre so fraught with rules (the dramatic unities, the rules of *vraisemblance* and *bienséance*, and so on—see Chapter 3 of this study) and limits? Both in terms of the dramatic form and in terms of the dramatic content of a play such as *Le Cid,* we need to keep in mind that the aesthetics of the classical theatre are linked to the nature of life at court— a concentration of nobles, intellectuals, and administrators at Versailles. The monarchy exerted its power by ordering the codes of behavior in this society: it was a very regulated life, full of interdictions and dangers to the individual and his personal freedom. Yet, this very society was looked up to by all France—indeed, by the world—as the center of luxury, delicacy, and refinement. In a world so full of regulations, the smallest act of etiquette or rebelliousness could cause shudders of excitement; after all, the aesthetic appreciation of any classical discipline depends on the notion of maintaining a high level of difficulties while yet conquering the difficulties with style and grace.

For France as a whole, long racked by disorder, this penchant for order and regulation was no doubt welcome; for the nobles, it was an unwelcome end to their independence and license. As Henry Carrington Lancaster writes: "It is quite natural that, after the disorders of the Wars of Religion and the revolts that preceded Richelieu's rule, Frenchmen should seek unity and regulation in government, social usage, literature, and art. It is not surprising that the society that produced the French Academy, Richelieu, Mme de Rambouillet, Malherbe, Guez de Balzac, and Poussin, should welcome plays written to accord with certain principles. The applause awarded to plays that kept the unities echoed that which greeted other political and social phenomena of the times. It is also quite comprehensible that there should be opposition to dramatic rules, just as there was to the power of Richelieu and Mazarin."[19] This spirit of opposition is very notably present in Corneille, both in his opposition to literary regulation (see Chapter 5 on the "Quarrel of *Le Cid*") as well as in the fabric of *Le Cid* itself.

As Lancaster notes further: "Although supposed to take place during the Middle Ages, the plot represents the manners of Corneille's times, with wars and dueling, clan spirit, and the growing influence of women. There is certainly no Richelieu, but the King is not unlike Louis XIII, while the rebellious nobles are represented by the Count, the loyal supporters of monarchy by the other male characters. The repulse of the Moors from the capital could not have failed to rouse memories of the recent driving of the Spaniards from Corbie."[20] Similarly, Georges Couton has suggested that *Le Cid* evokes the feudal mores of contemporary France, the vassal-like world of the *grandes maisons* with their political independence, the joy of the victory at Corbie, and the politics of dueling under Richelieu.[21]

The nobles' hatred of Richelieu and Mazarin and of the repressive measures of the monarchy would eventually result in that long, violent, traumatic, and unsuccessful series of upheavals known as the Fronde; it is only natural, then, as Bénichou suggests, that the age of Corneille and of the Fronde was "accompanied by a long spasm, undoubtedly the last, of feudal sensibility."[22] Ceertainly the notion of a great hero who is outside the rules—a notion dear to the feudal-baronic sensibility—is implicit in *Le Cid*, in spite of Corneille's own overtly constant obedience to Richelieu. The ethics of all of Corneille's plays are based on aristocratic pride in one's own glory and nobility, regardless of royalty. The Count of Gormas, Chimène's father, can, with fair accuracy, claim that the King and the realm depend on him and his martial prowess (lines 199–200, 376–82). When Don Arias warns him: "But kings demand a power that's absolute," his response is one of fierce individualism and pride: "The die is cast and I am resolute" (lines 387–88). For in the heroic code of values, personal honor exerts a greater authority and sway than obedience to the King; as the Count explains to Arias:

> When questions of esteem, sir, come along,
> Some disobedience is no great wrong
>
> (365–66)

Surely such lines must have been heavily charged with meaning to Corneille's aristocratic audience.[23] While clearly the Count is depicted as erring on the side of insubordination, nevertheless Corneille allows his duel with Rodrigue, a duel the King and Don Arias are unable to prevent, to seem a righteous and appropriate *affaire d'honneur*—despite Richelieu's interdiction against dueling. Later in the play, Chimène invokes the old tradition of justice through single combat between champions—a tradition the King dislikes, but must accede to in view of its popular acceptance. This image of a softer, benevolent King acceding to the wishes of his courtiers must have been delicious nostalgia for the aristocratic audiences but an undesirable and unfortunate depiction in the eyes of Richelieu. Rodrigue's own heroic license—like Corneille's seeming obedience to Richelieu—is different from the Count's only in word but not in deed: after killing the Count, his own heroic stature is such that he assembles an army at once without the King's authority and defeats the Moors on his own; is such that he can kill a father and marry his daughter with the King's approval; is such that the King himself admits to Chimène that Rodrigue is outside the Law:

> So I would
> Exempt Rodrigue: he is too dear to expose
> To fate's caprice and fortune's fickle blows;
> Such a great man's crime, be it what it may,
> Is, by the Moors in flight, now borne away
>
> (1410–14)

Rodrigue's very title of *Cid*, meaning lord, puts him on a plane equal to that of kings; he is a heroic demigod whom even a princess like the Infante can love without feeling loss of pride and station:

> Though I am meant for one of royal grade,
> Rodrigue, I'll live with pride under your reign.
>   The two kings in your train
>   Have you a monarch made.
> Does not this great name, Cid, which now you gain,
> Show clearly over whom you ought to reign?
>
> (1583–88)
>
> I love the man who's done such wondrous things—
> The valiant Cid, the master of two kings.
>
> (1635–36)

Rodrigue literally replaces the Count—in terms of both stature and heroic license—fulfilling Don Diègue's encouragement to him:

> Go fight, and show the King what you can do;
> Show him the Count was nothing: he has *you*.
>
> (1099–1100)

As Bénichou notes: "Horror of any humiliation to the ego is certainly the source of all valor in Corneille. . . . A sense of one's own worth, the approval of the public, and glory—these are the values in open conflict with the ideal of obedience."[24] Critics have speculated about the causes for Richelieu's alleged hostility to *Le Cid*—including perhaps Corneille's own pride which would not submit to the Cardinal's control over literary matters.[25] But whether or not Richelieu resented the play, certainly *Le Cid* was steeped in sentiments which, as Bénichou writes, "had little sympathy for the Cardinal's political methods. In fact the play is full of aphorisms which, in spite of their abstract quality, could be taken as a condemnation of Richelieu's politics. . . . *Le Cid*, with its uncompromising code on duels, honor, and redress by arms, with its two single combats, one as glorious as the other for the hero, and with its atmosphere of pride and insubordination, had nothing that could serve Richelieu's purposes with the public."[26]

In Richelieu's attempt to assert his power over the fiercely proud nobles, the prohibition against dueling (established in 1626, and punishable by execution) played an especially notable role. To begin with, it was of course a test of strength: "It meant stripping the lords of the last symbol of that autonomy they had once possessed; it meant teaching them that from then on only the king could bear arms and only he could settle their quarrels."[27] But far more than a mere test of strength, the prohibition of dueling interfered with a tradition sacred to the nobleman's code of honor and independence, for it was his sole means of redressing or saving his personal honor and glory, which (as with Corneille's heroes) were the defining qualities of a *grande âme*. As such, the duel—which the King tries to prevent in act 2 of *Le Cid*—is a sacred institution accepted by the aristocracy as part of its code which upholds personal honor as the highest of values; in *Le Cid*, even Chimène has to acknowledge that Rodrigue was right to kill her father, that she esteems him the more for his having done so, and that she could not esteem or love him any longer had he not tried to do so. Thus, in banning dueling, Richelieu had set up a conflict between personal freedom/honor/ pride and the absolute monarchy. The result was a spate of plots against the Cardinal which confirmed the aristocracy's prodigious hatred of the despotic prime minister.

Nor was dueling merely a cherished tradition that in practice was largely symbolic. In the last decade of Henri IV's reign alone, four thousand lords were killed in duels. Given the importance, then, of such affairs to the contemporary audience forced to submit their aristocratic honor to royal prohibition and control, *Le Cid* roused the passions of its audience through its political undercurrents as much as through its romanesque qualities and love interest.

What was Corneille's stance on the issue? In *Le Cid* the Count, Don Sanche, Don Diègue, and even Rodrigue himself seem to assert to various degrees the independence of heroic license (exemplified by the right to single combat)—while the subservient Don Arias alone seems to uphold the absolute power of the King. Four outspoken lines of the Count's in 2.1 originally presented an apology for dueling—but Corneille was forced to remove them, no doubt at Richelieu's insistence:

> *Ces satisfactions n'apaisent point une âme:*
> *Qui les reçoit n'a rien, qui les fait se diffame,*
> *Et de pareils accords l'effet le plus commun*
> *Est de perdre d'honneur deux hommes au lieu d'un.*

("These [royal] appeasements do not satisfy the soul: / He who receives them has nothing, he who makes them defames himself; / And in such agreements the most common result / Is the loss of honor for two men rather than one.")[28] When Chimène in 2.8, learning of her father's death, falls to her knees before the King and pleads her case to him as the arbiter in matters of personal justice—"A king must act when subjects' blood is spent"—Don Diègue's defiant reply to the King denies the crown any authority in such matters: "A just revenge deserves no punishment" (653–54). On the other hand, Corneille allows the King to make two condemnations of dueling as being detrimental to the welfare of the kingdom (lines 595–98 and 1405–10). Nevertheless, the King does not apply his will strictly, and is forced to admit the legitimacy and justice of the vengeance exacted by Rodrigue in killing the Count, and he grants royal approval to the combat between Rodrigue and Don Sanche (as Chimène's champion). Don Fernand is a portrait of the sort of good-natured, compliant monarch the French nobles would have liked to have had, or perhaps even imagined that they would have had without Richelieu.

Corneille later explained in the *Examen du Cid* (1660): "I believed myself justified in making [Don Fernand, the King in *Le Cid*] more compliant than would be the case in our times, when the king's authority is more absolute."[29] Thus Corneille could defend himself against any charges of insubordination by claiming that he was writing about eleventh-century Spain and not seventeenth-century France, despite the obviously inflammatory content of *Le Cid*'s political commentary. By that time, however, the last gasps of feudal insurgency had been crushed in the Fronde and *L'Etat c'est moi* would soon become a confirmed reality in the reign of Louis XIV (1661); some of the compelling immediacy of the political undercurrents in the play were inevitably lost to an audience now accustomed to the notion of royal absolutism as an unchallenged fact of life.

3

The French Theatre at the Time of *Le Cid*

The classical tragedy is often considered the finest expression of the spirit and genius of seventeenth-century France. Jacques Schérer makes high claims, in his *La Dramaturgie classique en France*, for the classical tragedy along these lines:

> It was in seventeenth-century France that the most complex plots were actually woven into a single action; henceforth a play did not merely tell a story, it had a subject. . . . In seventeenth-century France an attempt was made to attain that final perfection of literature, as Mallarmé was to call it, the elimination of chance, each entrance and exit being for a reason, each action down to the smallest details being governed by a likelihood, and both credible and necessary. In short, it was at that time that men brought to the theatrical art all the ornaments of good writing, poetry, rhetoric, style, at times, indeed, with excessive abundance. It was in France that writers made of the theatre their main or sole means of expression, so that the result on the stage was both first-class drama and an authentic expression of the national genius.[1]

Schérer's claims are large ones, yet not unusual ones among Frenchmen. And yet, while Molière's comedies have always found receptive audiences in the Anglo-Saxon world, the tragic works of the French classical period have long been a puzzle to the English mind.[2] While Frenchmen view the classical tragedy as the brightest moment in their literary tradition, English readers often see nothing there but highly artificial conventions, based on strict dramatic rules and unities, static tableaux in which no "drama" occurs beyond elegant declamation and rhetoric; the English mind does not understand that to the French these are masterpieces of dramatic *imagination* (rather than dramatic realism), compelling case-studies of passions depicted under carefully regulated conditions. Although *Le Cid* was a tragicomedy written before the form and essence of the classical tragedy had been rigorously defined—and thus was much more romanesque and baroque, and more flexible in its application of the rules—nevertheless, being a work in the tragic mode, it can only be understood within the context of French classical tragedy; in fact, the critical controversy which followed *Le Cid* helped define the form of classical tragedy. It is important for the English reader and playgoer to understand and to accept the most fundamental concepts and premises on which such plays are based.

In France poetry and drama became increasingly the province of an élite society which defined its own rules, based on principles of decorum, reason, order, and clarity. As Martin Turnell points out, "English literature was a literature of expansion and French a literature of concentration and consolidation."[3] In a society obsessed by rules and order, it was "the existence of authority that gives the literature its external order and its internal tension. . . . The whole tendency of the century was to express itself in brief, pithy maxims. . . . There was an unceasing effort to translate more and more of human experience into formulas, to reclaim it from the vast hinterland which lay just beyond 'reason' and 'good sense' "; as opposed to its English counterpart, French poetic drama "was not a voyage of discovery into the Unknown; it was a minute exploration of a known reality which can best be described as an *approfondissement* [a deepening] of everyday experience. The literary forms chosen by poets and prose-writers—the alexandrine, the maxim and the character—were used both as an intellectual discipline and to present complex material in the most lucid and orderly manner possible."[4] Most often the plays depict a struggle between reason and passion, between that ordered rationality and authority which the entire century aspired to, and the driving passions which make up the drama of human life. Each play becomes a concentrated case study of a particular version of that struggle.

"The sort of play we call classical," writes Will G. Moore, is "a play which relies for its effect on regularity of form, on unity of impression, and on absence of physical action. In it we expect to enjoy words and not to watch fisticuffs. Conflicts there are, as in all drama, but mental rather than physical, symbolic rather than realist."[5] And Georges May has defined the concept of tragedy developed by midcentury in France as: "a serious five-act play, written in an elevated style and in alexandrines [twelve-syllable lines]; with protagonists of noble blood engaged in a significant action, at least one of whom loses his life by the time the play ends."[6] One may quibble somewhat with this definition, but in Corneille's tragic works we invariably find a noble character, engaged in noble actions, struggling with his fate and his passions.

Whereas the English audience happily accepted a mixture of styles and tones within the same play, the French focused on one thing at a time: a tragedy had to be elevated in tone, sublime in language and expression, charged with stylized rhetoric and verbal wit (for example, "My greatest hope is but to hope no more"). Through the intense compression that comes with verse, and by eliminating most staged physical action, the compelling feature—and the crowning glory—of French classical drama became its marvelous use of *language*—of eloquence and rhetoric—as its primary dramatic vehicle. A sensitivity toward the subtleties and elegance of fine speech and sublime language is necessary for both the understanding and the appreciation of the classical stage.

As always, the ultimate purpose seems to be ordered concentration and focus. Moore writes about the classical drama:

> Every feature of classical drama is designed to offer a new kind of pleasure, a pleasure greater than realistic forms can offer. Its stylized language is more suggestive, not less, than everyday speech. Its rhetoric and its verse suggest more, and not less, than prosaic language can do. Its stress on credibility *(vraisemblance)* and on taste *(bienséance)* are meant to remove features which might shock and hinder us from entering fully into a most carefully designed illusion. The unities are means of concentration, of increasing our pleasure in the essence of an encounter or a mental state, by removing contingent and disturbing factors of time and place and irrelevance.[7]

What, then, were these rules and unities which governed such concentrated verse drama? Before we look at the development of such drama up to the time of *Le Cid*, let us first outline the celebrated but oft-misunderstood rules of the tragic stage to which the playwrights were attempting to conform, and which—following the Quarrel over *Le Cid* and the examples of Corneille's *Horace, Cinna,* and *Polyeucte*—became a formal definition of the genre.

The Rules *(Les Règles)*

In an age and a courtly society in which the key word was *règles* (rules) and in which all facets of life were ruled by absolutist authority, literature, too, required a submission by the authors to a set of rules and limits. Thus the century grew to prefer pure classical tragedy—so highly regulated, so beset by difficulties and challenges—as its essential genre, rather than more flexible forms such as romance, pastoral, and comedy. The genre, based to some degree on a misreading of Aristotle's unities and of Greek tragic models, was "classical" in the sense that "classicism" is a discipline involving the observation of rules, difficulties, and limits—and the overcoming of these with style and grace. It was thus a genre of limits, literary prohibitions sanctioned by Richelieu and by the Academy.

However, these rules were largely defined not by the dramatists themselves but by academic critics—*les doctes* or *les savants* (the learned), as they were called—in despite sometimes of the audience's preferences, and often in ignorance of the realities of theatrical staging and of successful dramatic writing. And so, as with any set of rules, there was a tension and opposition between the practicing dramatists themselves and the theorist *doctes*. Corneille himself never took an open stance of revolt and defiance (as did Molière) to the savants; but, unlike Racine, he did not merely accept the rules of tragic drama either, but empirically modified them somewhat—both in the practice of his plays and in the theory expounded in his essays on dramaturgy. In fact, it was *Le Cid* and the controversy aroused over its departures from the rules that first brought these issues to a head, and caused the rules to be formally decreed in principle by the Academy in 1637; and it was Corneille's three quintessential tragedies in 1640–42 (*Horace, Cinna,* and *Polyeucte*) which, by shifting to greater regularity in order to please the learned, solidified for the French popular taste the definitive form of the classical tragedy to be inherited by Racine and later tragedians. For Corneille was greatly popular with the audiences if not always with the critics.

In the decade before *Le Cid*, there had been much discussion about the merits and disadvantages of the *règles*. After the Quarrel and Corneille's three pure tragedies, the rules had won out—imposed on (and in spite of) the public taste by the *doctes,* with the support of the Academy, the salons, and Richelieu, all of whom wanted to control public taste and to have a theatre geared for the cultivated class *(les gens cultivés)* rather than for the general populace, known as *les ignorants.* With its lofty tone and its *grandes passions* and motives, the classical tragedy was, as Antoine Adam writes, "decidedly the dramatic form which suited people in a monarchic society, who recognized as reason for action only virtue and ambition, and who behaved only with high intentions" (my translation).[8]

In this tendency toward regularity which Richelieu and the Academy supported, the dramatists learned (in Lancaster's description of the nature of the genre) "to apply the classical ideas of restricting and unifying their subject, analyzing motives, preparing for an important action, holding the audience in suspense, leading up to the main event, and ending the play as soon as the unfinished business was over. . . . [They] also excluded the comic and bloodshed from tragedy. . . . The tendency to motivate entrances and exits responded to critical demands. The prevailing use of alexandrine verse corresponded to that of the iambic trimeter [of Greek and Roman drama], while the division into five acts bore the stamp of Horace's approval."[9]

The rules themselves can be conveniently divided into four categories: (1) rules defining tone; (2) rules of classical austerity (the unities); (3) rules of detail and decorum; (4) rules of verisimilitude and good taste.

1. *Tone.* A tragedy has to have the loftiest tone, to be an exercise in

sublimity of language and sentiment. (A) Noble characters: the characters have to be nobles of royal or heroic stature (the bourgeois were relegated to comedy) or figures from Greek and Roman antiquity (Pompey, Cinna, and so on). (B) The dramatic conflicts have to involve high passions such as love, power, vengeance, ambition, pride—these were the only sorts of topics allowed (rather than less "heroic" issues such as money, lust, and hunger). (C) Naturally the heroes of these tragedies would be *les grandes âmes,* great spirits with hubristic pride and larger-than-life passions.[10] (D) And a high tragic tone must always be maintained. Aristotle had suggested that tragedies should move audiences via terror and pity. In a classical scheme there is hardly room for the sort of comedy and low style which punctuated Elizabethan and Jacobean English tragedies. A scene in Racine's *Andromaque* which contained some dramatic irony and comedy at the expense of Pyrrhus caused audiences to laugh—and was universally deplored by the critics, for any laughs (especially at a heroic character) were a breach of the essence of tragic tone and loftiness.

2. *Rules of austerity.* Although the dramatic unities have often been equated with the *règles,* in fact they were only a part—and some of the least disputed—of *les règles.* The three dramatic unities were thought (or misinterpreted) to be Aristotle's doctrine of the drama as formulated in his *Poetics.* (A) Unity of time: the entire action of the play was to take place in the course of a single day (loosely defined as twenty-four hours). (B) Unity of place: the entire action was to take place in a single locale. The application of this rule gradually grew more strict—from a town to a palace and finally to a single site. Because of the harsh difficulty this unity presented in convening characters together plausibly, often the stage represented an abstract location, such as a palace antichamber (rather than, say, a specific character's chamber). The ostensible purpose of the unities of time and place was to avoid unseemly violations of verisimilitude—such as a character progressing from childhood to old age in the course of five acts in two hours, or of the stage representing Rome one moment and Egypt the next. But, in truth, such a motive seems rather absurd, since the entire notion of theatre itself is a convention, a lie, a fancy; we are not watching a literal mirror to nature but a shared suspension of disbelief. In fact, the rigors of the unities often caused greater violations of plausibility by forcing authors to cram a highly improbable number of dramatic occurrences into twenty-four hours or into a single physical location. Indeed, the actual and more useful purpose of the unities seems to have been for the effects of simplicity and austerity, so as to concentrate on the essences of a drama and not on digressions or subplots. Such was clearly the case with the third unity, (C) Unity of action: the play should be the development of one single story, unified by internal action, free of irrelevant or implausible intrusions or coincidences. In *Le Cid,* for example, most of the action seems to follow organically and be motivated by the situation of

two lovers whose fathers quarrel; but how was Corneille logically to fit in the battle with the Moors? In an effort to maintain the unity of place and time, he moved the action from Burgos (in the Spanish sources) to Seville, so that he could have the Moors sail up the Guadalquivir River and attack on the same day and at the same place of the action proper. But the unity of action is still violated, for there is still no clear connection to the main story, no internal logic or cohesion: the Arabs simply appear to fall out of the sky conveniently so that Rodrigue may become a warrior hero. Corneille later apologized for this, unconvincingly rationalizing that perhaps the Arabs wanted to take advantage of the Count's death to attack the weakened Castilian forces. (D) To the unities we can also add *la liaison de scène*, the continuity of scene and action: the stage should never be left empty. Act and scene divisions were usually defined by the logically or plausibly motivated entrance or exit of a character.

3. *Rules of detail and decorum.* These were a loose set of practical guidelines, not clearly distinguishable from the principles of lofty tone, verisimilitude, and good taste. (A) There was to be no mention of material objects and other vulgarities—knives, forks, and so on (one did not measure out one's life with coffee spoons, on the French stage). Only certain parts of the body could be mentioned, notably the carriers of emotions or symbolic connotations: face, eyes, forehead, hair, mouth, arm, hands, head, heart. Furniture and elaborate décor were to be avoided; a chair was acceptable. Other acceptable props and physical objects were swords, daggers, crowns, and scepters; but the presence of and dramatic weight attached to the handkerchief in *Othello* were considered in shockingly bad taste. (B) No violence or physical actions/conflicts were to take place on stage; the emphasis is on human emotions and discourse: dramatic action replaces physical action, in the forms of dialogue and monologue. Even the single action climaxing the fathers' argument in *Le Cid*—the celebrated slap the Count gives Don Diègue—was criticized; as Antoine Adam writes, "The Count's slap, in *Le Cid*, would be impossible to imagine in a [strict] tragedy" (my translation).[11] Motivations, not murders, were the focal interests.

Consequently, there was a heavy emphasis on monologues, in which a character could explose his/her deepest thoughts and feelings. To avoid an overpreponderance of monologues, writers learned to provide a major character with a confidant(e): this was a servant, friend, or follower *(suivant)* attached to the character and to whom the character could confide his innermost thoughts; the confidant was, in contrast, of the garden variety of human, and not himself or herself a tragic character. The practice of having confidants grew almost into a dramatic convention. (In *Le Cid*, Elvire and Léonor are examples of confidantes.) Similarly, another popular practice was to have *stances*, or stanzas; *stances*, an occasional dramatic monologue in elaborate stanzaic structure (as opposed to the staple alexandrine-couplet form), were in fact a relatively modern theatrical practice in France (and thus not sanctioned by the example of antiquity), but were frequently adopted as an ornate and challenging variation of the internal monologue. In *Le Cid*, there are two examples of *stances,* first by Rodrigue (1.6) and later by the Infante (5.2); Rodrigue's justly celebrated *stances* have been a particularly focal point of critical discussion, since much of his character, motives, and priorities may be discerned in this stanzaic deliberation over whether or not to avenge his father and honor and thus to kill the father of the woman he loves.

Since, however, noble passions and ambitions sometimes do involve battle, vengeance, murder, and so on, but since such violent action could not be played out on stage, the classical drama evolved yet another practice—called *le récit,* the recitation by one of the characters (often a minor character) of action which took place offstage. This small interior genre became so popular as to become almost a tradition: a tragedy must contain a *récit.* In *Le Cid,* the *récit* is in 4.3, in which Rodrigue himself narrates the events of the noctural battle with the Moors.

4. Finally, there are the related principles of verisimilitude, propriety, and good taste which we might collectively call the proprieties. Verisimilitude *(vraisemblance)* may be the most important element of the classical doctrine, for the unities, the observances of tone, and the issues of morality all have as their primary function the goal of providing plausibility. The Abbé d'Aubignac, in his *La Pratique du théâtre* (1657), set down in writing what had long been the accepted crucial principle of *vraisemblance,* or verisimilitude, as the key essence of the classical drama: the purpose of dramatic presentation is not to portray *le vrai* (the true) but *le vraisemblable* (the plausible and reasonable). Wedded not only to the unity of action but to the related ideals of *bon goût* (good taste) and *bienséance* (propriety), this was the form of ideal reality—a sort of higher reality than the real—which the classical drama was to assume. As d'Aubignac wrote: *"le vrai n'est pas le sujet de théâtre, parce qu'il y a bien des choses véritables qui n'y doivent pas être vues . . . qui pourtant seraient ridicules et peu croyables"* ("The true is not the subject of the stage, because there are many real things which should not be seen there . . . which however would be ridiculous and hard to believe").[12] The distinction is between the real and the realistic. The action of a play should not only seem to derive logically and reasonably from the situation depicted, but should do so in a seemly and tasteful way—since violence, outrages, and coincidence were considered *invraisemblable,* unreasonable or unrealistic. Thus, the issues of good taste and propriety subtly creep in under the aegis of verisimilitude, along with the moral utility which they imply. As Herbert Fogel points out (citing Scudéry, Boileau, La Bruyère, d'Aubignac, and others): "The three most important elements of the [classical] doctrine were that a play should be both useful and pleasing; that it should be likely or

believable; that it should be moral and have a moral aim. The century was almost unanimous in agreeing that the dramatic poem should convey a lesson."[13] It was largely over the issue of *vraisemblance* (with its related overtones of taste, propriety, and moral aim) that every critical controversy of the century was fought; *vraisemblance, bienséance,* and immorality were certainly the crucial issues in the "Quarrel of *Le Cid,*" as we shall later see. (For example, one of Scudéry's and Chapelain's main criticisms of the play was that it was shocking, and thus implausible, that Chimène could be so immoral as to wed the killer of her father; Chapelain's proposed suggestion—some elaborate resolution in which the Count either is found to be really alive or not to have been her real father after all—is even more ludicrously implausible.) The various didactic corollaries (the realistic over the real; virtue rewarded and crime punished) surrounding verisimilitude were ones that Corneille, despite the criticisms of the Academy, could never quite embrace, and he later expressed his objections to them, arguing that the main purpose of art and thus of any dramatic rules should be to please (see Chapter 5 on the "Quarrel" and other critical controversies).

Whereas in actual practice Corneille would bend his application of the rules in favor of dramaturgical effect, nevertheless he recognized their basic usefulness in forcing the dramatist to concentrate the dramatic action. Thus, despite the criticism he received over infractions of the rules and despite his own opposition to some of them, Corneille—through both his own practice (in the plays) and theory (in his essays and *examens* on dramaturgy) shaped and modified the acceptable rules of tragic drama—so that in 1738 Fontenelle could write in his *"Vie de Corneille"* that "Thus Mr. Corneille, through the study of Aristotle and Horace, through his own practice, through his reflections, and even more through his genius, found the true rules of dramatic poetry, and discovered the sources of the beautiful, which he then revealed to the whole world in the essays which preface his plays" (my translation).[14] As one of Corneille's contemporaries, a young man on Richelieu's staff named Desmarets de Saint-Sorlin, amusingly suggested in one of his own plays (*Les Visionnaires,* also successfully staged at the Marais, about a month or so after *Le Cid*), referring to the strict observance of rules and unities, the real purpose of this sort of concentration is to remove all extraneous distractions from the spectator and to focus his mind on the essence of a compressed dramatic action:

> *Il faut poser le jour, le lieu qu'on veut choisir*
> *Ce qui vous interrompt ôte tout le plaisir.*
> *Tout changement détruit cette agréable idée*
> *Et le fil délicat dont votre âme est guidée*
> *Si l'on voit qu'un sujet se passe en plus d'un jour,*
> *L'auteur, dit-on alors, m'a fait un mauvais tour;*

Il m'a fait sans dormir passez des nuits entières,
Excusez le pauvre homme, il a trop de matières.[15]

("One must present a day, a place which one must choose; / Whatever interrupts you strips away all your pleasure. / Any such change destroys this agreeable notion / And the delicate thread by which your soul has been led. / If you see that a story takes place in more than one day, / The author, you then say, has played a nasty trick on me; / He has made me pass entire nights without sleep; / Forgive the poor man, he has much too much material.")

The Development of French Tragic Drama up to *Le Cid*

In tracing the development of French dramatic literature in "the years 1635–1651, when the theater became, for the first time in modern France, the principal vehicle of literary expression," the great dramaturgical scholar Henry Carrington Lancaster comments that "Corneille succeeded in giving dramatic expression, as no one else had done in France, to the ideals of his age."[16] In a sense, however, Corneille's plays not only reflected his age but melded the different strains of French drama over the previous centuries into several plays whose success and genius gave impetus to and shaped what would become known as the French classic theatre.

In the sixteenth century, there were two general types of drama in France: a popular drama descended from medieval mysteries and farces, and a more learned drama. Dramatists in the latter group, influenced by Renaissance humanism, wrote plays based on classical models, especially Senecan tragedy. These writers—such as Jodelle, de la Taille, Garnier, Montchrétien—were the fathers of modern French tragedy. Unfortunately, these scholarly plays were more literary than dramatic, and worked better when read by a cultivated audience than when actually staged before an audience; these plays were largely suites of declamation, bare of dramatic action, whose major subject was the plight of man crushed by fate. As Peter H. Nurse writes: "Instead of a dramatic conflict of wills and a struggle to dominate Fate, we have in fact a succession of elegiac tableaux that exploit the pathos of human misery. . . . Faguet was not exaggerating when he described the majority of figures of sixteenth-century French tragedy as 'bouches parlantes' [talking mouths], rather than real complex characters of flesh and blood."[17] But these declamatory plays did establish the tradition, based on Classical models, which centers its dramatic impact on a concentrated rhetorical investigation of tragic misery rather than in the staging of physical or violent action; already the unities of time, place, and action were being largely observed. These plays of classical imitation became popular with the aristocracy, and were a cruder and more stylized foretaste of seventeenth-century tragic drama, centered more on pity and pathos than on the tragic.

But a new artistic sensibility had spread through Europe by the end of the sixteenth century—the baroque. Whereas classicism functions within a world of rational faculties and formal, ordered limits, the baroque spirit represented energy, disorder, and the passionate emotions which characterize the romanesque. In consequence, baroque drama was a modern theatre of conflict, allowing for individualistic and emotional characters, human interest in a variety of emotions, and intricate plots (often from Spanish and Italian sources) filled with suspense and staged (often violent) action; the emphasis in tragedy shifted from pity to horror. The unities were much more loosely observed. Eventually, the baroque and the sensibilities of the popular romanesque novels as well as of the salons of the *précieuses* resulted in the popularity of a modern genre, the *tragi-comédie*—plays with characters in both comic and tragic situations, more lax in observing the unities since they involved intricate plots with many dramatic twists and reversals. The tragicomedy reached its height of popularity between 1625 and 1630.

At just the same time, however, with the ascendancy of Richelieu and the growing sensibility of order and authority, and with the increasing control of popular taste by a cultured élite centered at court and in the salons, the *doctes* began reasserting the importance of the rules and the classical unities; thus began the critical controversy between the Ancients and the Moderns, or between the Regulars and the Irregulars—as they were called—which was to dominate the aesthetic discussions for the entire century. But even as the Ancients and formal tragedy regained the upper hand, the dramatists of this "regular" tragedy showed that they had learned a lesson: classic tragedy, while still concentrating action in rhetorical analysis rather than in physical action, incorporated now suspense and dramatic conflicts, manifesting a tragic struggle against Fate rather than merely an elegiac plaint of pathos and passivity.[18]

The interest in drama was growing, especially in the upper class. (One should realize that most Parisians never got to see a play, since the only permanent theatre at the time, the Hôtel de Bourgogne, could only seat less than 500 at a time.)[19] Richelieu's presence was instrumental in the development of the drama: his own patronage of the genre made it profitable to be an actor or a dramatist, fostering the conditions necessary for growth. He formed and employed the "Five Authors" (including Corneille) to compose plays with royal support; he had gala performances of successful plays put on at the Hôtel de Richelieu; he pensioned and supported Corneille, Mairet, Montdory, and others; he was deeply interested (and involved) in the Quarrel of *Le Cid* and the scholarly controversies of the day; he may even have helped compose some plays; and he built the finest theatre in France at that time, the Palais Cardinal. As with every development in his day, Richelieu played a major role; Lancaster writes that "without him, France could scarcely have acquired the prosperity needed for the improvement of its drama, in which he certainly took a very considerable and personal interest."[20]

In 1621, the formal renting of the Hôtel de Bourgogne by its theatrical troupe had established Paris's first permanent theatre. In December 1634, a second house—the Théâtre du Marais—opened, housing the company of the already famous actor Montdory. In addition to these two major theatres, there were occasionally special performances arranged at the Louvre and at the Petit-Bourbon; and in 1637 Richelieu completed the luxurious Palais-Royal theatre (the Palais Cardinal, or Hôtel de Richelieu). The Bourgogne and the Marais were rectangular and thus inconvenient for viewing; the Palais-Royal introduced an improved, semicircular, amphitheatre-like structure. The stage was still rather rudimentary in the two main theatres, with fairly simple scenery, the *mise en scène* usually a single view—a street, a garden, an antechamber. The scenery needed for *Le Cid*, Lancaster suggests, "was probably limited to a palace at the back of the stage and the house of one of the rival families on either side of it."[21]

The two theatres usually held performances three times a week. A typical evening's fare would include a comic prologue and the main five-act drama (tragedy, tragicomedy, or comedy), capped off by a farce. Later, when more severe tastes and rules had been sanctified (about 1640), the prologue and the farce were dispensed with, eliminating the mixture of genres—despite the fact that the popular audience had long been drawn to the theatre by these.[22] However, by then the drama had become the favorite entertainment of the ruling class. Of the two theatres, the Bourgogne was always the leading troupe, although the popularity of both Montdory and Corneille (who wrote his plays for the Marais) as the leading actor and the leading dramatist of the day kept the Marais a close rival. Corneille usually made sure his plays had fitting and large parts for the more celebrated stars of the troupe, Montdory and the two female leads, La Beaupré and La Beauchasteau (the presence of the latter may partly account for the role of the Infante in *Le Cid*).

As previously mentioned, in the 1630s the current popularity of tragicomedy over tragedy was somewhat stemmed by a revival of interest in Aristotle and Horace; the emphasis on unity and concentration of effect was revived; and the rules were successfully applied in several plays that turned out to be very successful. As the rule-oriented influence of Chapelain and other critics rose, the drama began to adopt the discipline of the unities; Corneille, who at the time was just one among a number of leading playwrights, provided a working model of a "regular" play in 1631, with his tragicomedy *Clitandre*. The subsequent success in 1634 of Rotrou's *Hercule mourant* and especially of Mairet's *Sophonisbe* marked the beginnings of the emergence of formal classical tragedy—respecting the unities, with subjects drawn from Classical sources, devoid of all nontragic matter, and excluding multiple plots and physical violence. The impact of *Sophonisbe* (acted by Montdory) was substantial. The next two seasons saw fourteen new tragedies, including ones by Scudéry, Rotrou, and Du Ryer; most were written in this new style, complying with the rules. But it was the success of Tristan L'Hermite's *Mariane* at the Marais in 1636 that confirmed the rising currency of the "regular" tragedy, and which shaped the dramatic *zeitgeist* and influences under which *Le Cid* was fashioned. "It is in this context that *Le Cid* should be read and imagined: a context of intense dramatic experiment, a new theatre, a new company, a new type of play."[23] Meanwhile, tragicomedies, much more lax with the new rules, remained popular: "The plays [tragicomedies] emphasize action at the expense of character, draw their leading persons from the aristocracy, show comparative freedom in structure and a happy ending. There is much that is extraordinary, but little that is supernatural. Though killing on the stage is rare, fighting is frequent."[24] In 1635 and 1636, there were about as many new tragicomedies produced as tragedies.

And then, at the beginning of 1637, appeared a play which took Paris by storm, whose brilliant success confirmed the new system and the future direction of French drama: this was *Le Cid*. For, though it was less regular than *Sophonisbe*, it was a play that generally conformed to the rules; and the critical dispute (the Quarrel) in its wake would bring the issue of the rules out into open debate and would legitimize them formally as the preferred critical taste. Most of all, it was a work of such phenomenal popularity that it became the focal point of discussion and imitation, the budding signal for the flowering of the literary age known as the French classical period. Enchanted by its rhetorical magic and moved by its human conflict of contrary obligations, everywhere in Paris people recited lines from the play to each other; Richelieu had it played twice at his palace; the play became the standard of admiration ("That is lovely, like *Le Cid*"); the text of the play was published almost immediately, and by the end of the year an English translation appeared and was performed in London.[25] As Lancaster writes: "Despite the [earlier] efforts of such writers as Mairet and Tristan, no permanent *chef-d'oeuvre* had appeared. This honor was reserved for Corneille, who now brought out one of the most popular plays ever written in France, a work that is the earliest classical monument of its century and the first modern French play to win recognition as a genuine contribution to world literature."[26]

Le Cid, writes Moore, "represents the realization of a form after which so many dramatists had been seeking, in so many ways, for nearly a hundred years"—a master play fusing together various elements and merits: "the idea of honour, the romanesque, the conflict of personalities, the psychological subtleties revealed by the verse form, the Alexandrine which can be as prosaic and informative as it can be rhythmical and suggestive. . . . It is perhaps the perfection of tragicomedy."[27] Although Corneille in 1648—at a time when tragicomedies were no longer in vogue or considered as respectable as the formal, "regular" tragedy—retitled *Le Cid* a "tragedy" (rather than the original "tragicomedy"), the play is clearly a tragicomedy (and is usually so titled now) but one which adheres to the new fashion, following Mairet and Tristan, of being a "regular" drama. As Adam reminds us, the play realizes the essence of the tragicomic form, a genre whose spirit is the romanesque: inspired by a Spanish (rather than Classical) story, its melodramatic situation involving the killing of the father of one's beloved was a frequent and dear one to the romantic and tragicomic tradition; like most tragicomedies, it was a bit flexible with the rules—containing secondary plots (the Infante, Don Sanche, the Moors) and a unity of place that admitted various locales within Seville.[28] Lancaster writes: "the struggle contains a tragic element in that the lovers find themselves both oppressed and inspired by the code [of honor], which plays the role of ancient Fate, but, as the play was called a tragi-comedy, the author, when enough sacrifice had been made to Honor, allowed Love to triumph."[29] Yet, while *Le Cid* is a human tragicomedy in the mode of the theatre of the baroque, the play contains a tragic dignity and moral seriousness that no previous tragicomedy could match. As Nurse observes: "A perfect example of the tragicomedy in its *romanesque* theme, with two duels and a battle between the Spaniards and the Moors to provide a constant source of excitement, the play also had the essential virtues of classical tragedy, for while its plot was undoubtedly colorful, almost all physical action was kept off the stage and the real drama based on the psychological conflicts of the two protagonists, Rodrigue and Chimène. The question is therefore: why did the play encounter such opposition from the partisans of neo-Classical theory?"[30]

As we shall see in the chapter on the Quarrel, the ensuing dispute centered not so much on the unities but on the proprieties—the rules of *vraisemblance* and *bienséance;* but the subsequent quarrel would bring all the issues of the rules to a head. Still, no one denied the power of *Le Cid* to move: all France loved the play, and only the academicians, quibbling over the rules, were displeased. As Lancaster reasons, "Both Romanticists and Classicists must have felt the dramatic effect of [the] struggle, first in the soul of Rodrigue, then in that of Chimène, the realization that the two enemies were lovers and that the heroism of each sustained the other."[31] The play's success was so tremendous that, in addition to its regular performances at the

Marais, it was shown thrice at the Louvre and twice at the Hôtel de Richelieu; it inspired three separate sequels by imitators.[32]

At the Marais, *Le Cid* was performed with Montdory as Rodrigue, La Villiers as Chimène, and La Beauchasteau as the Infante; soon it was also put on at the Bourgogne. Later, Molière's troupe would also stage it several times. Lancaster points out that at the Comédie Française it was the most frequently performed of all Corneille's plays between 1680 and 1900, having been put on 919 times by 1900; "No other play written in the first half of the seventeenth century has a record approaching this."[33] In our century, it has continued to be a staple production on the French stage (the Comédie Française alone staged it 506 times between 1900 and 1963),[34] with the best-known production being perhaps the 1951 performance at the Théâtre Nationale Populaire, starring Gérard Philipe and Françoise Spira.

In the wake of the Quarrel of *Le Cid*, the official and academic favoring of the rules became obvious. When Corneille introduced *Horace*, *Cinna*, and *Polyeucte* during 1640 to 1642, he confirmed this tendency, observing all rules and unities. As Lancaster writes, "If Mairet introduced the rules into French drama, . . . Corneille with his three great tragedies established the rules still more definitely, making possible their stricter and more general application to the plays of 1640–1651."[35] The Fronde (in 1648–53), however, brought this period of dramatic history to an end; during these years of national turmoil and humiliation, the theatres were closed for several months and the number of tragedies and tragicomedies produced fell drastically. Afterward, it was comedy that was increasingly the genre of popular preference and which seemed to reflect the national spirit; as Lancaster suggests, "Laughter seemed to be the only consolation for national affliction and disgrace."[36]

4

Le Cid: The Conflict of Love and Honor

Sources

Spanish tastes and fashions were very much in vogue in France during the early seventeenth century, and numerous tragicomedies and *précieux* novels found their inspirations in Spanish materials. Thus it is not surprising that Corneille would be taken by a play (published 1618) by the Spanish dramatist Guillèn de Castro (1569–1631), *Las Mocedades del Cid* ("The Youthful Exploits of the Cid"), and use it as the basis for a drama of his own.

The Cid was a figure in history and legend long before de Castro, however; he is the most popular hero in medieval Spanish legend. Actual historical details are few. There appears to have been a nobleman of Castile in eleventh-century Spain named Rodrigo de Bivar (1040?–99) who, having perhaps grown too powerful for comfort, was exiled by the king. Rodrigo and his men then put their services at the disposal of rival realms, even attacking his former king and country. Late in life, he conquered the Moorish stronghold of Valencia; the Arabs named him the "Cid" (lord) out of fear and respect. He had a wife named Ximena, daughter of a Count, whom he had apparently married for political reasons.

In subsequent years (after Rodrigo's death), the Spanish, long in fear of the hated Moorish invaders, saw much of their land (including Valencia) fall to these enemies again. Legend consequently chose to glorify the hero who had been once so feared by the Arabs, forgetting his earlier sins against Spain. The "Poem of the Cid" in the twelfth century, singing Rodrigo's exploits, was followed by other ballads and romances. The legend grew that Rodrigo had married, on the king's orders, the daughter of a man he had killed, as restitution to the orphan whose sole support he had removed. Then in 1601 a priest named Juan Mariana wrote a history of Spain in which he recorded a version of the legend in which it was Ximena, after her father's death, who demanded that Rodrigo should marry her, so as to replace the source of protection now lost to her.

Since such a version seemed, to the current courtly ideals of chivalry, a rather unromantic basis for a marriage, de Castro added his own innovation: Ximena loved Rodrigo even before her father's death; but afterward, rather than demand Rodrigo's hand in marriage, she demanded his death instead so as to avenge her honor. The seed for a complex and subtle conflict between love and honor had been planted. But in de Castro's hands this essential conflict is not given the focus of concentration, nor is there much care or attention paid to motive. In fact, de Castro's dramatic poem is more of a chronicle-play, long and rambling, involving events covering an eighteen-month span and a great deal of Spanish geography. Claude Abraham describes it as a "long, rambling dramatic poem in which the tragic rubs elbows with the comic, the trivial with the epic, and the tasteless with the sublime."[1] It also contained a number of what Lancaster calls "curiously naive scenes and picturesque encounters."[2] These included a scene in which the Count refers to Rodrigo's lips as still wet with his mother's milk, and another in which Don Diego, testing the relative courage of his three sons, bites Rodrigo's finger (the latter reacts, to Don Diego's satisfaction, with anger and violence, unlike his brothers). These barbarisms were hardly material that would be tolerated by a cultivated French audience eschewing staged violence and expecting *vraisemblance* and *bienséance.*

Corneille's version streamlines the tale to its essential conflict, and the play in his hands becomes a masterpiece of both dramatic presentation and sublime poetry. He eliminates the Cid's other exploits, focusing on the central conflict involving Chimène's love; he removes subplots and many unnecessary minor characters (the queen, the prince, Don Diègue's other two sons, a shepherd, a fencing instructor, and a leper!); he keeps the soldiers and the Arabs offstage; he eliminates or modifies any details which would have offended his audience's expectations of taste and verisimilitude; he keeps only those scenes essential to the play's central problem, and adds several that intensify the poignancy of the hero's and heroine's dilemmas; and he, more or less, "regularizes" the play in accordance with the recent trend and taste set by plays (like Mairet's *Sophonisbe*) which adhered to the unities.

In Corneille's play, there are only five major characters: Rodrigue, Chimène, Don Diègue, the King, and the Infante (the Count having been killed early in the play); Corneille makes the King weaker and more compliant than de Castro did, and he endows the Infante with a tragic grandeur by giving her an internal struggle—between love and honor—which parallels those of the two protagonists. Besides a number of new scenes added for dramatic preparation or for greater suspense, some of Corneille's additions are among the most crucial or celebrated sections of the play: Rodrigue's *stances* in 1.6 (in which his motives are analyzed); the King's objections to dueling; the King's decree that Chimène will wed Rodrigue if Rodrigue wins the duel (thus not only providing a more dramatic impact to the combat, but also removing the potentially controversial barbarism of Chimène's legendary demand and motives for marrying her husband's killer);[3] Rodrigue's second visit to Chimène's house (5.1) in which she admits that she would like to see him victorious; and the Infante's *stances* (5.2), in which she struggles with the need to renounce her love for Rodrigue in favor of her honor. Close to half of Corneille's play is wholly new material.[4]

Corneille's version of the play establishes classical order and structure, while keeping the romanesque attraction of a moving conflict involving love and honor. By eliminating secondary plots and focusing the action, he generally preserves the unity of action. He moves the action to Seville, so as to be able to present the battle with the Moors without violating the unities of time and place. More notably, he provides the play with a streamlined structure and five-act symmetry, whose very center is the key scene of Corneille's version, that first encounter in Chimène's house between the two lovers (3.4). And there are many symmetries of situation in the play—the two offstage duels, so fatal to Chimène's peace; the two encounters in Chimène's house; the foreshadowing of Chimène's later mistaking (5.5) of the situation when (in 4.5) she momentarily believes Rodrigue to have been killed—all of which accentuate and accelerate the dramatic impact of the denouement.

And so, while *Le Cid*'s spirit, human conflict, and dramatic peripeties are romanesque and tragicomic in essence, Corneille, by eliminating the mixed styles, subplots, and physical action common with tragicomedies, wrote a play whose concentration of focus and tragic grandeur provided it with a form and a dignity befitting the classical tragedy—a form whose currency was rising but which had not yet been fully defined. In doing so, as Lancaster writes, Corneille had

> perceived better than his predecessors had done what was to be the chief dramatic value of French classical plays. He realized that he had found in de Castro's work an excellent subject for his purposes, but he also saw that it was necessary to prune away picturesque and illogical elements, unnecessary characters and situations, to analyze more deeply the motives of the leading characters, and to concentrate his powers upon the development of the inner struggle of Rodrigue and Chimène. *Le Cid* became in his hands essentially the dramatization of a conflict between them and within them.[5]

The two elements in this conflict are Honor and Love—and it is to this conflict that we shall next turn our attention, after the summary below.

The following is Corneille's version of the story of the Cid, in brief summary:

The play, in five acts, is set in the Spanish court at Seville in the eleventh century. It is a tale of honor, courage, and love: both protagonists, Rodrigue and Chimène, must struggle with a difficult conflict of values, a conflict between their love for each other and their filial duties/responsibilities as demanded by their society's rigorous code of honor.

Rodrigue and Chimène, young and fine-spirited, are in love with each other. In the first act, Chimène is happy with the expectation that her father, the Count of Gormas, a great warrior and Spain's military bulwark, will look favorably on Rodrigue as a suitor for her hand. Unfortunately, the Count and Rodrigue's father, old Don Diègue—himself formerly Spain's greatest warrior—engage in an argument. The Count inadvisedly strikes the old man, an act demanding vengeance. Don Diègue exhorts young Rodrigue to this filial duty. Rodrigue is momentarily paralyzed by the conflicting demands of love and honor; but he chooses to preserve the family name.

In act 2, Rodrigue, despite being untried in combat, challenges the formidable Count to a duel—and kills the Count (offstage). Chimène, speaking with her friend the Infante (the King's daughter, herself secretly in love with Rodrigue), learns of her father's death; Chimène is now faced with a similar conflict—between her love for Rodrique and her duty to her own father. She chooses, like Rodrigue, to pursue her honor, clamoring to the King for vengeance against Rodrigue—while Don Diègue pleads to the King for mercy for his son's justified action.

In act 3, Rodrigue appears in secrecy before Chimène to offer up his life so as to satisfy her honor, now that his own vengeance is done; but both still love each other, and she refuses to take his life. Chimène is forced to admit that, although she must and will seek his death through the King's justice, pursuing her own duty and honor, she loves him still—and does not wish to see him dead. Meanwhile, the feared Moors have attacked the city; Don Diègue encourages his son to show the King that the great warrior Count will not be missed. Rodrigue will secretly lead an army of men to face the enemy.

In act 4, Rodrigue and his men have routed the Moors (offstage, in an all-night battle); the King welcomes warmly the nation's new hero (replacing the Count) and pardons him his vengeance against the Count. Chimène's only recourse now is to invoke the tradition of single combat, offering her hand in marriage to any champion who will slay Rodrigue in fair combat; the King, frowning on this ancient custom, reluctantly agrees—but, suspecting that she still loves Rodrigue, stipulates that the victor, *whoever* it be, will win Chimène as wife. Don Sanche, a brave courtier enamored of Chimène, takes up the challenge against Rodrigue.

In act 5, again Rodrigue appears before Chimène to give up his life; again Chimène can only admit that her own desires clash with the duty she is pursuing, and that she wishes him to be the victor in the duel. Thus inspired, Rodrigue defeats Don Sanche easily. Meanwhile, the Infante renounces her love for Rodrigue so as to maintain her honor and her peace of mind. Don Sanche appears before Chimène with a bloodied sword, for Rodrigue has spared his life and sent him to Chimène with the news. But Chimène, mistaking the outcome momentarily, reveals now openly her grief and love for Rodrigue. Then, realizing her mistake, she again demands vengeance. The King, satisfied that she truly loves Rodrigue, decrees that Rodrigue will lead his armies into battle while Chimène mourns her father, but that Rodrigue, on his return, will finally wed his true love, whom the King will console and pacify in the meantime.

La Gloire: The Heroic Ideal of Honor

Corneille's plays have frequently been interpreted according to what Fogel refers to as "the legend that depicts Cornelian tragedy as the conflict between duty and passion and the subjugation of passions to nobler sentiments."[6] In such a scheme, the purpose appears to be the glorification of the will. But that is a misreading of the plays, for Corneille's plays—especially *Le Cid*—are not so much dramas of duty or dramas of will as they are dramas of *passion*. In the values of Corneille's age, the highest passion and human faculty was *la gloire:* one's sense of glory, pride, honor, fame, esteem. And so, rather than a conflict between duty and passion, *Le Cid* depicts a struggle between two different but similarly compelling passions—*la gloire* and *l'amour*, honor and love. In fact, the terms *devoir* (duty) and *volonté* (will) appear relatively infrequently in Corneille's plays, in contrast to *la gloire*, which is constantly invoked by the characters as the guiding force in their thoughts and actions.

Corneille's contemporaries during the reign of Richelieu and Louis XIII admired his plays for their ability to move the emotions of the audience, for *la gloire* was the valued passion they understood best, and it was the source of the sublime in Corneille's drama. As Paul Bénichou writes: "Passion in Corneille was entirely steeped in the atmosphere of aristocratic pride, glory, nobility and romance that pervaded France during the reign of Louis XIII, and permeated the entire literature of that epoch. Under Louis XIV, the sublime as Corneille had envisioned it already seemed a bit archaic."[7] With the destruction of the hopes of the *grands* in the Fronde and the formalization of the absolute monarchy under Louis XIV, the pride of the *grandes âmes* who had struggled against Richelieu was crushed, and the themes of individual and heroic greatness and self-worth seemed outmoded. "Deprived of its natural life and movement, Corneille's concept of the sublime ultimately drew itself up above the passions in frigid splendor. The *bien pensant* [straight-thinking] bourgeoisie of the nineteenth century was attracted to the notion of an almost puritanical Corneille, sublime in a bourgeois fashion by the value he placed on self-constraint and effort."[8] Thus, the energetic effort based on *la gloire* became misread as the basis for a moralizing literature of will and duty. Nineteenth-century critics such as Brunetière, Lemaître, and Lanson posited a reasoned will as the ruling force in the plays, eventually denying emotions as having any force in Corneille's work, always suborned by will and reason.[9]

Anyone who reads *Le Cid*, however, can see that the sense of honor which drives its characters is not a cold and moralistic sense of will, but a passionate emotion of the ego and its pride, unwilling to commit any acts unworthy of an *âme bien née* (a soul of noble birth). Honor and *gloire* form an emotion not only as warmly compelling as love, but more so, for love itself is dependent on one's sense of honor. In the hierarchy of passions, honor stands highest, for without his honor a *grande âme* like Rodrigue can neither love nor be loved. And to be honorably loved by a *grande âme* adds to one's own glory.

This great sense of self-worth and honor at any cost was admired by baroque and romanesque tastes as the distinguishing trait of the heroic ideal, the evidence of the most sublime spirit. Nurse writes that "It is this Baroque fascination for the morally ambivalent energy which raises man above his normal human limits that has earned for Corneille his reputation as the poet of Heroism."[10] For at the center of Cornelian values is the notion that heroism is not subject to universal rules or reason, but always aims to prove itself more glorious and more worthy, always affirming the value of the self, whether in the fields of battle, love, honor, or generosity. These heroes were great souls with large passions—all exceptional men with the highest ideals and energy. Antoine Adam argues that to understand this concept of heroism, we must discard the austere and frigid nineteenth-century bourgeois and puritanical notion of a universal moral Law which the will submits to; rather, the spirit of the time was filled with the highest heroic ideals and passions: "Here is the actual notion we should have of the Cornelian hero. He is not restrained by any law; he does not conform his behavior to the needs equally felt by the common man. He embraces with passionate energy the heroic task which faces him" (my translation).[11] And it is *la gloire* which motivates this energy and drive; as Adam writes further, "For precisely the reason that the Cornelian hero acts out of an appetite for glory and not because of a submission to a law, he is not the cold and insensible being which some have imagined. He is all passion. For to Corneille as to the Great Ones of his century, it belonged to the soul to be passionate."[12] Certainly Rodrigue is as passionate a hero as any Romantic sensibility could ask for.

While pride is the source of sin in Christian ethics, in heroic/aristocratic values it is the source of the sublime and of deserved admiration; Corneille's heroes are never humble. Rodrigue, before he has been even tested once in combat, can boast that

Men like myself don't need a second test.
My maiden strokes will match those of the best.

(409–10)

—for he is a well-born hero who believes in himself, and whose very sense of self-glory is of itself to be admired. The inspiration for such a glorification of the ego is the feudal ideal of the heroic; as we have seen, feudal ideals and courtly notions of love thrived at this period, "when favorable social conditions, the renewed prestige of the nobility, and political unrest created conditions for their most dazzling development. . . . we understand that a certain kind of passion, inseparable from the aristocratic tradition, inspired all of [Corneille's] heroes."[13]

In feudal/aristocratic ethics, one's only duty was neither to social nor to moral law, but to be worthy of oneself and one's lineage. One's ancestry and social station are the source of one's generous (as in the Latin *genus, generis*) pride. And any defamation of the family glory is the greatest insult possible to one's most valued faculty, one's personal pride and honor. Thus it is that a single slap on the face can set off a chain-reaction of combat, death, and vengeance. The ethos of generic pride of noble birth is described and explained early in the play by the Count himself, whose words are reported by Elvire to Chimène ironically only moments before he will insult Rodrigue's father:

> . . . Both [Sanche and Rodrigue] are men of worth,
> Being of noble and loyal blood by birth,
> Both young, but in their eyes I plainly see
> The valiant spirit of their ancestry.
> Rodrigue's features, especially, reveal
> The embodiment of the heroic ideal—
> A worthy son of a long lineage
> Teeming with mighty heroes, age to age.
>
> (25–32)

There are no greater imperatives than (and no ethical obstacles to) the defense of one's family honor when it is threatened; this is a view shared by all, the motive which drives all the characters. When, in his *stances,* Rodrigue momentarily contemplates not trying to kill Chimène's father, his reaction to the idea is one of instinctive, generic horror:

> To die thus unrevenged!
> And bring our family name such infamy!
> All Spain would impute to my memory
> The stigma of a house left unavenged!
>
> (331–34)

Similarly, when Chimène is faced with the choice of whether or not to avenge her own father, her decisiveness proves her own worth and glory, revealing the source of her motivation:

> My honor is at stake, I must avenge
> Myself; however much love may beguile,
> To noble souls all such excuse seems vile.
>
> (842–44)

[handwritten note: Find verse that Antigone uses to say the same thing]

Where honor is at stake, one must defend onself at any cost. This is such a universally acknowledged truth that, when violated, even a lowly hand-maiden is allowed rightfully to lecture a princess, as when Léonor reprimands the Infante:

> Forgive me, Madame, if I
> Speak openly, to say this love must die.
> How could a princess like yourself lose sight
> Of her own place, and love a common knight?
>
> (85–88)

In a heroic society, there is no answer to such a rebuke but to reaffirm one's honor, as the Infante does:

> But I'll defend the glory of my station,
> And fight desire with determination.
>
> (97–98)

What one inherits from one's lineage is pride, and the courage and daring which make one worthy of pride. "In what still survived of feudal society at that time," Bénichou writes,[14] "the supreme values were ambition, daring, and success. The weight of the sword and boldness in one's desire and speech constituted excellence; evil consisted in weakness or timidity, in the paucity of desire and daring, and in sustaining an offense without inflicting one in return—these were enough to exclude one from the ranks of the great and consign one to the common herd." In fact, from such pride comes every other faculty and emotion; in the argument between the Count and Don Diègue, the rivalry for glory and pride ends up very soon involving every passion—ambition, hatred, desire, resentment, defiance, anger, vengeance. As so often in the play, actual dueling and feudal jousts are replaced by a series of contests over the greater pride and glory: the Count and Don Diègue's argument; the challenges and boasts betwen Rodrigue and the Count; Chimène's and the Infante's rivalry for the glory of Rodrigue's love; Chimène's and Don Diègue's conflicting appeals for the King's justice; in a sense, the entire play (once the Count is killed) can be seen as a contest between Rodrigue and Chimène to see who is the most worthy of pride and honor, and thus who is most worthy of the other's love.

All of Corneille's major characters are marked by a lust for glory and greatness. Any hesitation or self-doubt is an admission of unheroic weakness. When Rodrigue wants to impress Chimène with just how shockingly strong his love for her is, he explains that it actually made him hestitate momentarily from the pursuit and defense of his honor: "*You* judge its power: despite the affronted state / My name stood in, I did deliberate" (881–82). Nor should this sense of pride be in fear of the danger of death, for a noble death adds exponentially to one's glory (a notion dear to every feudal ethos, whether Roman, Anglo-Saxon, samurai, or whatever), allowing one's fame to escape the bounds of any temporal reversal or demotion. This is why Cornelian heroes are so quick and willing to offer up their lives (as Rodrigue does to Chimène in 3.4 and 5.1), even if to us it may seem like gratuitous suicide, martyrdom, or folly; as Rodrigue explains, in any death that is a *beau geste*, a noble deed (whether in combat or in love), there can only result an increase in glory:

> Nothing's of greater worth to me than my
> Own honor. No, think what you will, but I
> Can die without risking my glory. . . .
> No, men will only say:. . . .
> "To avenge his honor he denied his heart;
> To avenge his mistress he then chose to part
> From life, from her, preferring, in this strife,
> His honor to Chimene, and her to life."
> So thus you'll see that my death in this fight
> Won't dim my glory, but make it more bright.
> From my glad death this honor will ensue:
> That none but I could have contented you.
>
>   (1528–46)

But such a refined *délicatesse* of romantic gesture—the honor of a death to content one's beloved (rather than the heroic death in combat)—is a notion of honor which neither Rodrigue's father nor Chimène's would have recognized, for Corneille has imbued their children not only with the inherited feudal/heroic warrior tradition, but also with the courtly love ideals made popular in Corneille's day by the baroque romances and the salons of the *précieuses*. But it is of love we are now speaking, and it is to that we turn our attention.

The Conflict of Love and Honor

For these two issues, Honor and Love, are hardly separable; in *Le Cid*, *gloire* dominates and enlightens love, and it is Corneille's originality to show that love can itself be a source of honor but, even more so, that honor is both the source and the domain of love.

In an aristocratic society, the feudal-heroic values of the warrior class are mingled with the more refined and chivalric values of courtly love. It is in Corneille's notion of love that the influence of the *précieuses* is most obvious: since love is founded on esteem and merit (in other words, on *gloire*), it is not a weakness but rather another type of glory, and a "perfect lover" is as much an object of admiration as a warrior covered with martial success. Inevitably a parallel is drawn between conquests in love and in war: as Bénichou explains, "There is a general tendency in the spirit of chivalry to make love a spur to greatness. Amorous conquest, with its rivalries, its difficulties, and its glory, imitated military conquests and could demand the same virtues."[15] In the courtly love tradition of the medieval ballads and romances, the woman becomes a powerful idol in a religion of love, able to command a knight's submission, obedience, and loyalty. His belligerence on the battlefield must be matched by his gentleness in the boudoir, always trying to please the lady. Thus it is that Rodrigue, who can defeat fearsome counts and countless Moors, offers up his life repeatedly to Chimène if that is what would please her or satisfy her honor. Even after he has "won" her as wife (by royal decree) in defeating Don Sanche, he will not take her in such ungentle fashion, but would defer to her wishes:

> I come not to collect my prize, Chimene,
> But to present my head to you again.
> Madame: my love for you does not require
> The law of combat nor the King's desire.
>
> (1777–80)

Gallant submission to a lady is a high priority in courtly ideals, and Rodrigue is no less a perfect knight than Lancelot.[16]

Robert J. Nelson very properly reminds us that the play is as much about love as about glory, the two passions which dominate the young lovers, starcrossed like Romeo and Juliet by a dispute between their houses: "Accustomed by centuries of criticism to the image of the 'Cornelian hero' in *Le Cid* we are liable to forget that the heroes of the play, Rodrigue *and* Chimène, are presented to us primarily not as heroes but as lovers. . . . Throughout the play the dramatist maintains in the spectator's breast a contrapuntal effect between the amorous and the moral in which the amorous is the dominant motif."[17] Dramatically speaking, the purpose of the duels, of the battle with the Moors, and of Rodrigue's sudden greatness—is not to cover Rodrigue with glory, but to make the play's treatment of love all the more poignant and affecting, in the conflict between love and honor these produce within Chimène: "Rodrigue's rise to power only serves the non-political purpose of making him seem at once more desirable and more detestable to his beloved enemy."[18]

Rodrigue's and Chimène's parallel conflicts between love and honor begin when their two fathers engage in an argument, in 1.3, over who is the proper tutor for the young prince of Castile. It is a contest over comparative worth and glory. Although their children's affection for each other is mentioned, both men are solely concerned about their honor and pride. To us today the scene may seem like a childish exercise in squabbling vanity—but such a sense of pride and self-worth was the aristocratic ideal of the age and the trait of tragic greatness. The actual progression of the argument, leading up to the insulting slap so fatal to the lovers' happiness, is a fine, stylized example of rhetorical pacing: the two men exchange long passages praising their respective merits, but, as the argument builds, they exchange (lines 215–24) ten heated lines (five apiece) of single-line statements; it *is* a duel: thrust, parry; charge, countercharge; bon mot, repartee. Finally, the lines build up in pace even into shared half-lines of stichomythia, climaxed by the slap:

> THE COUNT: In terms of courage, I deserve it most.
> DON DIEGUE: He who has lost does not deserve the post.
> THE COUNT: I don't deserve? I?
> DON DIEGUE: You.
> THE COUNT: Such impudence,
>   You bold dotard, will have its recompense.
> *(He slaps Don Diegue)*
>
> (223–26)

There is a marvelous linguistic effect here in the original French: the Count's action of striking is accompanied verbally by the insulting use of the familiar case of "you" (*toi*, as opposed to *vous*): *Ton impudence, / Téméraire vieillard, aura sa récompense* (Your impudence, bold dotard, shall have its recompense). To an audience versed in classical drama, sensitive to nuances of language as the dramatic action of the play, the Count's sharp and angry "*Ton*" (rather than than the respectful and expected "*votre*") was shock and insult enough; the physical slap merely confirmed the need for vengeance.

Lancaster points out that the proud Count, unwilling to submit himself to any law, "represents the turbulent princes of Corneille's day, and his downfall is a forerunner of theirs."[19] Don Sanche, who would have to be classified as another of these unruly barons, defends him by explaining to the King why he cannot submit to the King's punishment:

> one accustomed to great acts cannot
> Lower himself to the debasing thought
> Of such submission without feeling shame.
> That's what he fears, and that's what is to blame.
>
> (583–86)

The preference, as always for men like the Count, lies in action and strength:

> Order his arm, nourished by valiant action,
> To prove his cause; he'll give full satisfaction
> At sword's point; order that, and he'll obey.
>
> (589–91)

Don Diègue's values are much the same, and together the two fathers represent the heroic warrior ethos of the feudal tradition, living by the sword. While Corneille forgoes the Spanish version that has Don Diègue at this point biting Rodrigue's finger to test his courage, the famous 1.5 serves much the same purpose in words if not in barbaric action. Rodrigue walks onstage for the first time, and Don Diègue's test question *Rodrigue, as-tu du coeur?* ("Do you have courage?") is immediately answered with a choleric arrogance which pleases his father:

> DON DIEGUE: Rodrigue, speak: are you brave?
> RODRIGUE: I'll send him who
> Dares doubt it to his grave.
> DON DIEGUE: Well said! Such true
> Resolve is music to my troubled ears.
> The family spirit thrives in you and nears
> The proud perfection of my younger days.
> Come, then, my son, my blood, and earn my praise,
> Come and avenge me.
>
> (261–67)

(Abraham suggests that "The drama of *Le Cid* does not really begin until Don Diègue asks the famous question: 'Rodrigue, have you courage?' ")[20] Don Diègue, satisfied that Rodrigue has the spirit required, urges him on with the warrior ethos, *meurs ou tue* (kill or be killed):

> Kill or be killed, for blood alone can free
> Our pride.
>
> (275–76)

He knows Rodrigue loves Chimène, but (in a famous maxim: *Mais qui peut vivre infâme est indigne du jour*) he reminds his son that

> Yes, I know your love—so don't reply;
> But live in shame and you deserve to die.
>
> (283–84)

"His is a simple soul," Lancaster writes, "intensely emotional, untouched by modern conceptions of love."[21] Again and again, Don Diègue is quite willing to send his son to face a likely death—whether against the formidable Count, the feared Moors, or Don Sanche immediately after the all-night struggle with the Moors—all for glory.

But the choices for Rodrigue and Chimène are not so simple. For if the fathers stand for a simpler and older heroic ethos which their children also accept, the younger generation, however, has its own and new imperative: they adhere simultaneously to the new values of love in the courtly tradition (and in the seventeenth-century French salons). When father and son meet again, Rodrigue having killed the Count, the situation brings Don Diègue's simple mind unadulterated joy, but it evokes in Rodrigue a single "Alas!" (1026). The jubilation for one is a catastrophe for the other, since Rodrigue's love for Chimène is now doomed. Don Diègue is a throwback to the prechivalric tradition of feudal heroism, unable to understand or sympathize with the more complex motivation of his son, steeped in the courtly ideals of romantic love. The fathers' is a heroic cult of male virility, what Bénichou calls an "anti-love tradition" represented by such medieval heroes as Roland: "This anti-love tradition is often embodied in Corneille by the old people, particularly the fathers, the natural custodians of the healthy misogyny of earlier times. . . . It is they who teach contempt for woman, relegating love to the background, valuing only the glory of arms and the approval of men."[22]

And so, to Rodrigue's "Alas!" Don Diègue responds by urging him to rejoice in his victory over the Count and the glory he has brought himself and the family name. To his father's affirmation that he should

> now from such
> A noble heart cast out these weaknesses;
> We've but one honor—there are many mistresses!
> Love's but a joy—honor's a duty, though.
>
> (1056–59)

—Rodrigue can only cry out in incensed anguish, "What are you saying!" (1060) For, in courtly love values, love is more than a mere pleasure—it, too, *is* a duty, an imperative, a demanding religion. And so Rodrigue responds by educating his father in the courtly ideal:

> My injured honor wreaks revenge on me,
> And you dare urge me to infidelity!
> An equal shame follows the cowardly soldier
> And the unfaithful lover both. . . .
>
> (1061–64)

That last sentence reflects the equal place given to glory in the field of battle and honor in the field of love; as Abraham notes, "Here, simply stated, is the courtly ideal, . . . the simultaneous acceptance of contradictory obligations so familiar to readers of medieval romances."[23] We have a clash between systems of values—the warrior ethic and courtly love. In Rodrigue the two forces are equally balanced, and he will not compromise either one; he must be both the perfect hero and the perfect lover.[24] As Octave Nadal argues, this is a broadening of the feudal ideal—the model knight taking on not only the knightly ideals but the ethos of the perfect lover.[25] Rodrigue is the embodiment of both; but in choosing to be so, he must satisfy both imperatives. How does one do so when glory and love are in conflict?

We shall investigate in detail how both Rodrigue and Chimène try to satisfy both love and honor, but when Rodrigue later explains that he had to pursue his glory (thus renouncing his love) in order to deserve his love, he suggests that in fact he *can* reconcile the two, because both enter into the same hierarchy of values, in which glory is the highest. Love depends on worth, on being worthy to be loved. As Bénichou writes: "The formula he employs is very significant: '*Grandes âmes* should yield to love *only to the extent that love is compatible with nobler sentiments*'. . . . In Corneille there is no absolute opposition between love and that greatness which is the very stuff of the tragic theater. In all his works he tried to reconcile the two, rather than set them against one another."[26] It is life (and drama) that sets up such tragic conflicts; it is the stuff of tragicomedy to show how they can be happily resolved.

Rodrigue's Decision

Rodrigue's struggle with this conflict and the choice he makes is presented to us in his celebrated monologue of 1.6, popularly known as Rodrigue's *stances* (stanzas). These lyrical configurations—six elaborate but symmetrical ten-line stanzas, identical in shape and line-configuration, rhyming ABBACCDEDE—are a rhetorical artifice of highly stylized beauty, in which Rodrigue, raised to a fever pitch of emotional conflict, undergoes a moving internal struggle with the choices, equally vexing, facing him. *Stances* were a popular form of the period, often used to represent a focal moral struggle; Lancaster notes about Rodrigue's *stances* that the contemporary critic the abbé d'Aubignac "declares that they delighted all the court and all Paris, though, with extraordinary obtuseness, he objects to the fact that Rodrique is not given time to compose them!"[27]

Rodrigue's father has just left the scene with his famous line of exhortation *(va, cours, vole, et nous venge):* "Go, run, fly—avenge us now!" (290) No doubt a real hero in the mold of the fathers' generation would have had no hesitations or existential deliberations; the response should be immediate action. But left alone on the stage, Rodrigue's depression and paralyzed anguish contrast markedly with Don Diègue's energetic call to action:

> Oh, struck deep in my heart
> By a cruel blow unlooked for and acute,

> Wretched avenger in a just dispute,
> Unwilling pawn, yet bound to play the part,
> I remain rooted, and my troubled soul
>   Has lost control.
>   So close to having Chimene's hand—
>   Oh God, what pain!
>   The victim is my father, and
>   The offender, father of Chimene.
>
> (291–300)

Rodrigue does not resent the source of his wretchedness, for, embracing his father's heroic values and pride, he realizes it is a "just dispute" in which he is "bound to play the part" he owes his father. But it is the equally compelling demand of his love for Chimène—and what he owes her—that roots him in wretchedness and causes such pain; the appropriately repeated rhyme-pair in each stanza pits "pain" *(peine)* and "Chimene."

Rodrigue is all too aware of the harsh injustice of having *two* sets of values he must satisfy, and despite his impassioned anguish, he dissects the conflict accurately:

> Harsh and unjust demand!
> It pits my honor against my love; to obey
> A father, I must throw my love away.
> One spurs my pride, the other stays my hand.
> My choice is whether to betray love's flame,
>   Or live in shame;
>   Both ways I'm cursed forevermore.
>   Oh God, the pain!
>   Should I neglect my honor, or
>   Punish the father of Chimene?
>
> (301–10)

The dualistic symmetries in the lines themselves present a repeated balance ("One spurs my pride, the other stays my hand") between the competing demands of honor and love. "Should duty, or love, hold sway?" Rodrigue asks himself, "bound by just yet difficult constraints" (311–12); but what he realizes (unlike his father) is that love, too, is itself a duty: "My duty is also to Chimene" (322). Either way he will be forsaking a duty he owes; either way, he realizes, he will lose Chimène, incurring either her hatred or her scorn, for—and this is the key point—she subscribes to the same heroic code he does, and in fact would *expect* him to seek an honorable revenge; if he did not, he would prove himself unworthy of her love. Logically and analytically, it would then follow that Rodrigue should pursue his honor first, since his love depends on it in any case. But though he subconsciously realizes this (and though Rodrigue will later in 3.4 cite this motive as his logical reasoning), at this moment Rodrigue is more emotional than rational, and it only serves to increase his pains and make him consider ending his seemingly inevitable misery altogether through suicide—sinking into what Nadal calls "the double vertigo of voluptuousness and death":[28]

> Death might best end my pain.
> My duty is also to Chimene: this path
> Of vengeance would incur her hate and wrath.
> But to refrain would merit her disdain.
> Either I prove unfaithful, or a lover
>   Unworthy of her.
> Everything seems, whatever I try,
>   To increase my pain.
> Come now, my soul: since we must die,
> At least let's not offend Chimene.
>
>   (321–30)

The *stances* are not so much a rational process of logical deliberation and choice as an affective series of anguished emotions and impulses to which Rodrigue reacts. Having now sunk to the impulse of suicide, the next counterreaction is decisive: from deep in his gut suddenly rises the virile cry of the heroic warrior-class, remembering who he is in a burst of *grande passion:*

> To die thus unrevenged!
> And bring our family name such infamy!
> All Spain would impute to my memory
> The stigma of a house left unavenged!
>
>   (331–34)

Rodrigue rejects suicide out of the instinctual shame felt by a *grande âme* at the thought of a death with dishonor.[29]

And it is only now that he consciously rationalizes the logical realization that he has to pursue his honor just to retain Chimène's love, that by not doing so he would lose his worthiness and her respect—what Nelson calls "the paradox of love as honor."[30] Thus either way he would alienate Chimène:

> To seek a love which necessarily
>   Is lost to me!
> Heed such seductive thoughts no more—
>   They bring you pain.
> Salvage, at least, your honor, for
> In any case you'll lose Chimene.
>
>   (335–40)

The reasoning here is logical and compelling, and no doubt Rodrigue would
have arrived at it eventually—and so there is no hypocrisy when he later cites
to Chimène this paradox of love as honor as his motive for killing her father:
"I wronged you, but I had to, to preserve / Honor, to efface my shame, and
to deserve / Your love" (895–97). But in fact we see that the conclusive
moment of decision was based on a purely emotional response of humilia-
tion at any dishonor to the family name.

And so, having realized earlier that "My duty is also to Chimene," he now
returns to the more basic imperative on which Chimène's love itself de-
pends—personal honor and family reputation:

> Yes, love has blinded me.
> My duty's to my father: I'll defend
> The honor of our blood, whether I end
> My life in combat or in misery.
>
> (341–44)

And now Rodrigue realizes that a proper warrior-hero would have acted
immediately and not have hesitated in the first place:

> I move too slow! I must run to my fate,
> Not hesitate;
> Ashamed by such deliberation,
> I'll end my pain
> Avenging this humiliation
> Wrought by the father of Chimene.
>
> (345–50)

But the fact that he deliberates at all is due to his equal status as perfect lover,
and is testimony to the fervor of his love for Chimène. As Georges Couton
argues: "That he could take the time for deliberation and postponement of a
vengeance which imposed itself as a reflex, furnishes the most striking proof
of his passion for Chimène. . . . Stormy deliberation, more passionate than
rational. The most tumultuous and pathetic moment is here: the play would
not again reach such a tempestuous climax" (my translation).[31]

Thus, what appears at first to be a conflict between love and honor (since
the pursuit of honor would apparently prevent the realization of love) is,
given the paradox of love as honor, finally not a conflict at all. In the
hierarchy of values of the code shared by both lovers (and the society),
honor is highest, and love (and all other values) depend on the preservation
of honor. When honor comes first, all things should follow. If Rodrigue does
not avenge his father, he loses his glory and Chimène's esteem; he thus has
everything to lose. But if Rodrigue does avenge his father, he covers himself
in glory and, really, forces Chimène to love him all the more: thus he has

everything to gain. Although Rodrigue arrives at this choice through an anguish of emotional storm, it is the only choice possible for a noble and heroic spirit like his own. Like the English Cavalier poet Richard Lovelace, Rodrigue could claim that "I could not love thee, dear, so much / Loved I not honor more."[32]

Having taken the only viable route, Rodrigue can have no regrets, however painful the consequences; as he tells Chimène in 3.4, "[I] found him, then avenged my family name. / I'd do it again, if things were still the same" (877–78). Now shining in glory, Rodrigue can only seem *more* lovable to Chimène, not less; as she admits to Elvire: "More than just love: I *adore* Rodrigue" (810). Sharing the same values, Chimène cannot reproach him, but can only try in her turn to imitate and to equal him, proving her own self-worth according to their shared values and thus proving herself, in turn, worthy of him. This becomes the substance of 3.4, the most enduringly cherished and popular scene in the play.

Chimène's Decision

Rodrigue's critical decision is reached by the end of the first act and his vengeance accomplished halfway through the second. The rest of the play (including the offstage battle with the Moors, which makes Rodrigue even more worthy of love and less subject to royal punishment) is dramatically designed around the choice Chimène now faces and the ensuing issue of whether or not she will be able to accomplish her own vengeance and redeem her honor. (This led Emile Faguet to suggest that the play should really be titled *Chimène*.)[33] On that issue also hangs the romantic interest—whether or not the lovers will be reunited.

Chimène's plight is similar to Rodrigue's—a conflict between love and honor, involving the duty of avenging one's father and family name. In Chimène Rodrigue has the good fortune of encountering a soul every bit as noble and heroic as his own, constant in her romantic passion but upheld foremost by the imperative of *la gloire*. Unlike the Infante, who wavers through most of the play over which of these two imperatives to pursue (settling necessarily on honor only in act 5), Chimène—while never disowning her continued love for Rodrigue—instinctively and decisively, like Rodrigue, opts to pursue her honor. Rodrigue has set her the example of such behavior, and she must not show any weakness that would prove her to be any less worthy of esteem. Having seen her father's lifeless body on the ground, she rushes at once to the King to demand vengeance and Rodrigue's head (2.7), in an emotional plea for justice, appealing both to the King's sympathy and to his sense of justice—culminating with: "Murderers must die for justice to be done" (738). This sentiment doesn't prevent her from loving Rodrigue all the more and even admitting it to Rodrigue in their two conversations together; there is no contradiction here, for Chimène, at once proud and loving, is no more willing to concede the loss of either honor or love than was Rodrigue. In this she responds (and corresponds) to his spirit marvelously, and Corneille's delighted audiences could only romantically conclude that two souls of such fine excess were meant for each other.

The process of decision, then, is the same as Rodrigue's—an instinctive choice of honor over love, of father over beloved. This instinctive choice will become in 3.4 a conscious realization of the paradox of love as honor. Moments before that, in 3.3, even as she avows her love in confidence to Elvire ("More than just love: I *adore* Rodrigue") she does not hesitate (as did Rodrigue) in her plan of action:

> Whatever influence love has over me,
> I shall not hesitate: I clearly see
> My duty—I'll follow it implicitly.
> Although Rodrigue is very dear to me
> And though he owns my heart, yet in my head
> I know who I am, and that my father's dead.
>
> (819–26)

As she explains to Elvire, *il y va de ma gloire:* "My honor is at stake" (842); it is the highest imperative of the Cornelian stage. But if Chimène's choice is similar to Rodrigue's, her plight is even more pitiable than his. For whereas, as we saw, he had everything to gain by pursuing his vengeance—restored honor and the greater esteem of Chimène—she can only lose: in killing Rodrigue she restores her honor but also extinguishes the possibility of love altogether, ensuring the loss of *both* persons (lover and father) most dear to her. Given such tragic circumstances, her desire for self-immolation (but only after her glory has been avenged) is both more touching and more understandable than Rodrigue's; she tells Elvire her plan to

> Preserve my honor, end my pains, pursue
> My true love to his death, and then die, too.
>
> (847–48)

At this point Rodrigue reveals to her his presence in her house, as 3.4 opens: "Well, then! No need for more pursuit or strife: / You have the honor now to take my life" (849–50). Chimène's shocked reaction ("Elvire, where are we? What is it I see? / Rodrigue in my own house, in front of me!") is also the audience's, for this famous romanesque scene proved rather scandalous on a tragic stage. (The Academy would also criticize the immorality of the scene: how could Chimène allow her father's killer to talk to her in her own house?) As Nadal argues, this interview between the two protagonists presented an ingenuous scandal: "The night, the corpse within the house, this chamber in which the orphan has sought refuge in tears, and, suddenly Rodrigue in front of her, sword in hand—these savage images are pitched at the eyes at a time and at a place which, from all evidence, would deny them" (my translation).[34] Rodrigue's sword—which he offers Chimène to use to kill him—is, in Chimène's horrified words, "still dripping with my father's blood!" (858); it is a scene of extravagance and horror. And in spite of all this Rodrigue manages to elicit from her lips her love for him; is this much different in shock effect from Richard's seduction of Anne in the first act of *Richard the Third*? As Nadal concludes, the scene "approaches almost a hallucination."[35] But the public loved this scene, both for its stunning dramatic effect and for its romantic preciousness; and so Corneille kept it in later editions despite the critics' accusations that he violated both verisimilitude and propriety, and defended its dramatic value in his 1660 *Examen du Cid*.

It is in this celebrated encounter that Rodrigue now explains to Chimène his motivations. He begins by noting that he cannot regret any action made in defense of his honor:

> For you must not expect me to retract,
> Despite my love for you, a righteous act.
>
> (869–70)

He then confesses the hesitation we witnessed in his *stances*, making what to us today might seem a backhanded compliment to her power over him, but coming from a proud warrior in a heroic society it is a powerful avowal of the strength of his love for her:

> Not that my love for you did not, in fact,
> Struggle against my duty in this act.
> *You* judge its power: despite the affronted state
> My name stood in, I did deliberate.
>
> (879–82)

And it is here that he rationalizes to her the paradox of love as honor as his motive—which was certainly there, although his immediate decision, as we saw in the *stances*, was made based on instinctual fear of dishonor:

> And your great beauty
> Would certainly have turned me from my duty
> If I had not opposed it with this thought:
> That a dishonored man deserves you not,
> . . . that to heed Love's guileful voice
> Makes me unworthy, and defames your choice.
>
> . . . .

> I wronged you, but I had to, to preserve
> Honor, to efface my shame, and to deserve
> Your love. . . .

(885–97)

Having met his obligations to honor and to love, Rodrigue now offers up his life to Chimène. As Bénichou points out, "suicide for honor's sake, by one's own hand or with another's help"—which to us may seem mere folly—was to Corneille's contemporaries the essence of "*Bel-esprit*—subtle intelligence in search of beauty and grandeur . . . the most admired trait in all intellectual life."[36] In a sense, 3.4 can be read as a tournament of *bel-esprit* (fine-spiritedness), a duel between Rodrigue and Chimène for the greater generosity of noble spirit, as Chimène tries to match Rodrigue's greatness in honor. But the Academy in its *Sentiments* charged Rodrigue with hypocrisy for asking Chimène to take his life instead of taking it himself—was he really intending to die, or was this a calculated ploy (as in a seduction) to force from her a confession of love? But the Academy and Corneille's critics blatantly and repeatedly ignored both the emotional moment and the dramatic content of the scene. As Nelson argues, "in each instance where the Académie would have a monster of reflection we have only a dramatic character. The Académie demands too much presence of mind from the distraught Rodrigue and . . . has failed to grasp the dramatic excitement of his symbolic gesture (we post-Freudians and devotees of the Metaphysicals know all too well the strange alliance between Eros and Thanatos)."[37]

Chimène's reply is a masterpiece of symmetrical response and reciprocity, for what she must do now is try to satisfy—as he was able to—her honor without committing violence to her love. For, as Nelson accurately concludes, "The paradox of love as honor is that in the beloved the lover is only seeking an image of himself. Possession—of the self—is the very essence of love-as-honor."[38] And the first step in self-possession is to preserve one's own honor and sense of worth, to make sure it matches the beloved one's. She begins by admitting that she cannot reproach him for an action where his honor was at stake; rather, she must emulate him in this contest of fine spirits:

> You only did your duty as all fine
> Men should; in doing yours, you taught me mine.
> You avenged your father and upheld your name:
> Your valor shows me I must do the same.
> I have a father to avenge, like you;
> I have my honor to uphold now, too.

(911–16)

She parries his earlier thrust by echoing his own words in arguing that she, too, will not regret an act of honor, even when it means his death, for love doesn't alter the imperative of honor/vengeance:

And you must not expect me to retract,
Despite my love for you, this vengeful act.

(927–28; cf. 871–72)

She concludes her argument with a logic which to us today may ring with a delicious, Monty Pythonish silliness, but to an audience steeped in courtly traditions was the height of subtlety in *bel-esprit:*

Though love's persuasive, my nobility
Must correspond to yours. By wronging me,
You've proven worthy of me and done your due;
I must, by killing you, prove worthy of you.

(929–32)

As with the argument between the Count and Don Diègue in act 1, this duel of words and imitation progresses through increasingly shorter passages and accumulating pace, until it reaches the stage of stichomythia in Chimène's shameful admission (in line 963) that:

Then go—I hate you not.
RODRIGUE: You should.
CHIMENE: I can't.

At this point, our duel turns into a duet—which is only appropriate in an exchange between a duo of combatants who are, at once, foes and lovers. This justly celebrated duet, capping what Lancaster calls "a remarkable scene of analysis,"[39] comes at the very center of the play and is its lyrical climax and the high point of preciousness. At the duet's most poignant moment, Chimène's whispered confession that "though I / Obey such a cruel duty's rigorousness, / My one wish is to be quite powerless" (982–84) is followed by this famous lyrical exchange:

RODRIGUE: O miracle of love!
CHIMENE: O heavy pain!
RODRIGUE: What woes our fathers force on us, Chimene!
CHIMENE: Rodrigue, who would have known—
RODRIGUE: —or thought to say—
CHIMENE: That joy so near could so soon fly away?

(985–88)

By this point surely Corneille's enchanted audience realized, if it had not done so earlier, that these two lovers, who can even complete each other's very thoughts (and rhymes), are equally worthy of the other as models of the perfect lover in a heroic society. They must be allowed to love. And the rest of our tragicomedy unwinds the means by which a star-crossed marriage of true minds is allowed finally to realize a marriage of true love; it is a romantic resolution which was both demanded by the genre and which proved delightfully satisfactory to a charmed audience.

Coda: The Plight of Chimène

But if the duet suggests their equality in heroic perfection, it also reveals a marked contrast between the lovers' situations. Chimène's admission of her continued affection is to Rodrigue a "miracle of love" but to herself a "heavy pain." For Chimène's plight is intrinsically more hopeless and tragic than his; she is the more doleful and pained, because her dilemma is insoluble. Rodrigue could, in pursuing his honor, also increase Chimène's love for him; in killing the Count, he could in good conscience continue to love Chimène, for it was not Chimène who offended his honor. But Chimène cannot love so freely: she sees in Rodrigue's own person the hated murderer of her father and the object of her vengeance; thus, her love is both honorable (as it is for Rodrigue) and criminal (as the Academy would remind in overplus). She is, as Nadal says, filled with "an obscure feeling of culpability" (my translation).[40] Chimène's dilemma has a poignant pathos, because unlike Rodrigue she cannot love without feeling guilt and dishonor, and so her misery is inevitable, regardless of outcome:

> How should
> My sorrow be appeased if I can't hate
> The hand that caused the pain? What other fate
> Is mine but agony if I pursue
> A crime, yet love its perpetrator, too?
>
> (805–8)

Nor can the successful pursuit of her vengeance bring her any satisfaction—for, while such action brought Rodrigue restored honor and the knowledge that Chimène can only esteem him the more, such vengeance can only bring Chimène the extinction of the object of her love. Nevertheless, the heroic imperative is so strong and inflexible that neither love nor honor leaves her any choice but to seek vengeance and restore her honor:

> Though to him my heart is true,
> Though people praise him, and the King does, too,
> And though brave men surround him, none the less
> I'll crush his laurels beneath my cypresses.
>
> (1193–96)

Her pitiable dilemma has the potential for a tragic denouement in a tragedy titled *Chimène*.

But this is a tragicomedy titled *Le Cid,* and the rest of the play is a romantically "precious" skein of events building up to the final, happy resolution. The ending was not only popular with the public and its romanesque tastes, but seems onstage a dramatically appropriate joining of two lovers so deserving of each other in every way. It is only in later deliberation that one is struck by the play's injustices to Chimène, given the heroic priority of pursuit of honor. Not only do her two meetings with Rodrigue force her into unwilling and pained (since shameful) admissions of her continued love and of her wish that Rodrigue defeat Don Sanche (1547–57)—Nadal goes so far as to accuse Rodrigue of being a vainglorious and cruelly manipulative seducer seeking to satisfy his male ego[41]—her unsuccessful pursuit of vengeance is thwarted by what seems in a way an unplanned conspiracy by three men—Rodrigue, Don Diègue, and the King. For, by trying to be every bit as heroic as Rodrigue in pursuing her honor and vengeance, Chimène is playing at being a hero in a man's world—and she is simply not allowed to. Nevertheless, as Abraham notes, "Limited physically as a woman in a man's world, Chimène refuses to allow her conduct to be guided by these limitations"[42]—unlike the Infante, who, in "feminine" fashion, wavers precariously in the upholding of her honor. Despite her continued passion for Rodrigue, Chimène never hesitates. But whereas in the courtly tradition woman is idealized as the goddess to whom all obedience is due, she is not allowed to win in the lists of heroic competition.

The final resolution is possible only because Chimène is the victim of a male game played to deprive her of her "masculine" *gloire.* To begin with, the inequality of their respective plights forces her to flinch first in the pursuit of her duty, in her guilty admissions of her continued love for him; Rodrigue himself need feel no guilt in loving. She is shown to be still a "woman," evincing and admitting her emotions despite her primary desire to acquit herself honorably. One could even, like Nadal, argue that the only real purpose and explanation for Rodrigue's two visits to her house (since it is inconceivable that a great hero should actually die at the hands of a girl!) is cruelly to force her into shameful admissions of her continued but now dishonorable love for him. And Corneille's insertion of Rodrigue's conquest of the Moors at this moment allows the King to justify being unsympathetic to Chimène's pleas for justice, since Rodrigue has now proven himself a demigod indispensable to the national security, and beyond the reach of ordinary laws (a notion popular to the pre-Fronde *grands*). As the King tells him after the victory:

> I pardon you for avenging your offense.
> A rescued nation speaks in your defense:
> Henceforth be sure Chimene will speak in vain—
> I'll but console her if she speaks again.

> (1253–56)

By the time Chimène is announced as on her way to plead her case once more, she has become in the King's eyes now no more than a pest: "Annoying news! Unwelcome obligation!" (1331)

All circumstances conspire against Chimène's success in her *affaire d'honneur,* for at this point (4.5) Don Diègue tells the King that she also loves Rodrigue, and the King commands of everyone: "I shall test her will. Affect a sadder visage" (1336–37). With this comic, music-hall trick perpetrated by the entire male court, all wearing long faces and pretending that Rodrigue has died in battle, the King and Don Diègue are able to elicit from Chimène a swoon, for she truly believes Rodrigue is dead. She recovers admirably, claiming to have fainted from joy rather than grief. (But this test only foreshadows her later and irrecoverable display of grief in 5.5.) Then, when the King confronts her with "Consult your heart; Rodrigue is master there" (1391), Chimène's threatened honor desperately reacts by taking the offensive: she invokes the custom of single combat to redress her honor, promising her hand in marriage to whoever will kill Rodrigue in a duel; Don Sanche answers the call as her champion. But at this point the King conceives a diabolical idea: *whoever* wins will marry Chimène by royal decree.

> My hand shall then present him to Chimene;
> Her marriage vow shall be, then, his reward.
>
> (1458–59)

Reduced to a mere prize to be awarded in a contest of martial prowess, an object to be handed over to the killer of her father, Chimène can only scream in protest: "What a harsh law to impose on me, my lord!" (1460) The King answers her now as if she were a child whose claims are not to be taken seriously:

> Stop murmuring against such a sweet decree:
> You'll marry him who earns the victory.
>
> (1463–64)

It is a terrible situation for her: whatever happens, she must marry either her father's killer or her lover's killer; either way she loses.

Rodrigue's second (and equally shocking) visit to her chamber in 5.1 has the functional result of forcing Chimène—when Rodrigue threatens simply to let Don Sanche kill him—into a second admission even more pained and shameful than the first:

> Go and fight valiantly,
> To force my hand, to impose silence on me;
> If in your heart your love for me still lies,

> Then win this duel for which I am the prize.
> Adieu: these stray words make me blush with shame.
>
> (1553–57)

It is a startling moment of weakness on Chimène's part (Scudéry in his *Observations* called these words *dignes d'une prostituée*, "worthy of a prostitute"[43]), unwillingly forced on her, to her shameful anguish, by Rodrigue. But he in turn is instantly and fully regenerated ("And *now* what enemy can I not tame?" in line 1558): inspired by what is to her a moment of tortured wretchedness (one recalls "O miracle of love!" versus "O heavy pain!" in the first meeting's parallel moment), Rodrigue goes out and defeats Don Sanche easily.

Chimène's honor is finally undone in 5.5 by a second "trick," a coincidence that has the circumstantial quality of comedy: Don Sanche has been spared his life and is sent to Chimène carrying his sword, to announce Rodrigue's magnanimous victory. Just as she was forced to look at the bloody sword that slew her father, she now thinks she is looking at the sword that killed Rodrigue (and speaks a response parallel to the earlier instance: "What! and still dripping with my lover's blood!"—line 1706). Believing Rodrigue dead and her vengeance complete, she bursts forth in open grief and anger at Don Sanche (her refusal to listen to him smacks of comedy), avowing her love and no longer feeling a need to hide her emotions—only to learn in 5.5 that once again Rodrigue is still alive. But this time she has said too much to recover her honor. It is through such a series of tricks and circumstances that Chimène's pursuit of vengeance is at last terminated; unable any longer to deny her continued love for Rodrigue, she can only, in accepting the King's command, object to the unseemliness of being forced to wed the killer of one's father:

> If for
> The State Rodrigue's such a necessity,
> Must I for his deeds be the salary,
> Soiling eternally my own good name,
> My hands dipped in my father's blood and shame?
>
> (1809–12)

And so the King concedes her a reprieve during which Rodrigue will lead his armies to battle and after which delay the nuptials might seem more seemly ("What seems at first inexorable crime / Has oft been made legitimate through time"—1813–14). But even the play's ringing, final words are tinged somewhat with a condescending and paternalistic attitude, as the King assures Rodrigue that he will deal with Chimène's objections in the meantime:

> Hope in your courage, hope in my word, too;
> Your love's heart is already won by you;
> As to Chimene's continued wavering,
> Leave that to time, your valor, and your king.
>
>   (1837–40)

The reflections in the above "coda," however, are, admittedly, after-thoughts—dependent on a modern "feminist" literary consciousness—based on years of nevertheless enjoying the play's romantic idyll and its treatment of perfect love. Certainly the play is satisfying to one's romantic ideals and expectations, and the implied final union between Rodrigue and Chimène seems an only appropriate joining of two souls so noble and similar. In staged performance, particularly, the pleasing dramatic effect leaves no unsettling questions or aftertaste; the theatregoing public, enchanted and charmed by the fine excesses and delicacies of Rodrigue's and Chimène's sentiments, could only applaud the satisfying resolution of tragicomedy after witnessing two perfect lovers acquit themselves heroically—internally and externally—in an anguished and "tragic" struggle with the simultaneous demands of honor and of love.

5

"The Quarrel of *Le Cid*" and Other Critical Controversies

The Quarrel of *Le Cid*

The stunning and instantaneous triumph of *Le Cid* in 1637 seemed to be officially confirmed almost immediately: first by Richelieu's ennoblement of the Corneille family (the knighting of his father), and secondly by the play's becoming the center of a stormy and major critical controversy, the notorious *Querelle du Cid*. More than just a literary dispute, the Quarrel was the most significant critical discussion of the classical period, for it not only raised the aesthetic issues which would dominate French literature and criticism for the entire century and would color future French cultural tastes, but determined the course of French seventeenth-century theatre, which in 1637 was poised in an even balance between the taste for the theatre of the baroque and that for the "classic" theatre.[1]

In 1637 the tragicomedy was still perhaps the most popular dramatic genre, but, as we have seen, the renewed interest in classical "rules" had created a growing interest in "regular" tragedies such as Jean Mairet's successful *Sophonisbe* in 1634 and Tristan's *Mariane* in 1636. And now in January 1637 came Corneille's *Le Cid*, a tragicomedy which nevertheless adhered to the classical regulations; its smashing impact immediately raised Corneille, in the eyes of the public, to the position of France's foremost dramatist.

But if the admiration for the play was boundless with the public, it was less so in literary circles: the classicists felt that it was not quite regular enough, and fellow playwrights—once on an equal plane with Corneille—were now jealous of their rival's new glory and status. In this charged atmosphere Corneille committed two ingenuously unfortunate and mistimed acts of pride. First he had the play published almost immediately (successful plays were usually published months later), thus allowing for a close critical scrutiny of the text. And then, in February or March, he brought out a poem, which it seems he had written much earlier, titled *Excuse à Ariste,* in which—displaying all the vainglory of a Cornelian hero, even of Chimène's father the Count—he boasted of his superiority over all other dramatists and of his indebtedness to none. The poem includes these lines:

> *Je satisfaits ensemble et peuple et courtisans*
> *Et mes vers en tous lieux sont mes seuls partisans*
> *Par leur seule beauté ma plume est estimée*
> *Je ne dois qu'à moy seul toute ma Renommée,*
> *Et pense toute fois n'avoir point de rival*
> *A qui je fasse tort en le traittant d'égal.*[2]
>
> ("I please at once both the people and the courtiers, / And everywhere my verses are my only partisans: / For their beauty alone is my pen esteemed. / I owe to no one but myself all of my Renown / And always feel that I have no rival / Whom I would wrong by treating as an equal.")

Corneille may simply have meant here that his success was due not to courtier's influence or intrigue but to the intrinsic merits of his plays—but the poem could not have come at a more inappropriate time to stir up the resentments of fellow playwrights, especially Jean Mairet and Georges Scudéry.

What followed was a war of pamphlets. Stung by the *Excuse à Ariste,* Mairet—who had recently been praised for *Sophonisbe*—followed with a six-stanza poem supposedly written by "The Author of the real Spanish *El Cid* to his French translator," accusing Corneille of plagiarizing de Castro's play while claiming that his renown was owed only to himself. Corneille replied with an impertinent *rondeau,* insulting Mairet for being a *"fou solennel"* (solemn madman). Mairet retorted (in July) with his *Epistre familière,* claiming that the play's success was owed to de Castro and to the talents of the Marais actors; in return, as Lancaster puts it, "Corneille's friends attacked Mairet, casting aspersions upon his family and drawing from him a long account of his genealogy."[3]

Of less personal but more critically substantive interest were Scudéry's *Observations sur Le Cid,* which were published meanwhile in April. This was a detailed critical examination of the play, concluding:

> *Que le sujet n'en vaut rien du tout,*
> *Qu'il choque les principales règles du poème dramatique,*
> *Qu'il a beaucoup de méchants vers,*
> *Que presque tout ce qu'il a de beautés sont dérobées.*[4]

("That the subject is worthless; that it violates the principal rules of dramatic poetry; that it has many bad verses; that almost all of its beauties are stolen.")

The last charge is the issue—already raised by Mairet—of plagiarism from de Castro again. And the third charge was supported by a list of specific lines that seemed to Scudéry awkward in style, taste, or construction. But it is his discussion of the first two charges that is most significant, for Scudéry argued that the play violated the principles of verisimilitude and propriety. His list of violations of verisimilitude included: the number of events crowded into twenty-four hours; the Count's behavior and speech, which was more that of a *matamore* (braggart) or a *miles gloriosus* (braggartly soldier) than of a courtier; the presence of so many unnecessary characters, especially the Infante—a character he claimed was created in order to give a part to La Beauchasteau—and Don Sanche, who seemed to exist only so as to be beaten by Rodrigue. Other alleged violations claimed by Scudéry were of a finicky absurdness (along the lines of "How many children had Lady Macbeth?") and lacking in any suspension of disbelief; I quote Lancaster: "The king should have set guards to prevent the duel. Chimène should not be left without friends. Don Diègue is uncivil in leaving the 500 men at his house and this number is far too large. The king is disobeyed, is undignified when he tests the heroine's love, and unjust when he bids her marry the winner of the judicial combat. Moreover the harbor of Seville should have been closed with a chain; the Moors should not have cast anchor; the duel of Rodrigue and Sanche could not take place while only 140 lines were being spoken."[5]

But Scudéry's most telling point, despite the above inanities, had to do with the ethical principle of *bienséance*, propriety. Arguing that plays should instruct, Scudéry claimed that they thus had to be both verisimilar and morally proper. Chimène's continued love for her father's assassin was thus both improbable and shockingly immoral. She ought not to have approved of his actions against her father, and certainly not to admit that she loved him or that she wanted him to defeat Don Sanche. Such an admission, he claimed, was "worthy of a prostitute." In a play portraying the conflict between duty and love, he felt, Chimène's weakness and willingness to wed Rodrigue confirmed the immoral victory of love over duty.

Corneille's response was his *Lettre apologitique*, a masterpiece of irony in its self-effacement and praise of Scudéry; besides noting how popular the play was with the public, though, Corneille refused to be drawn into a substantive discussion. Others were less hesitant. Three anonymous pamphlets came out refuting Scudéry's arguments (the third also contained some new charges against *Le Cid*)—making, among other points, the significant arguments that "poetry is not to be regulated by critics, that the conduct of

Rodrigue and Chimène is justified by their love, that the Infanta's devotion to Rodrigue shows that Chimène's affections were directed towards a most worthy object."[6]

At this point the sheer number of pamphlets from both attackers and defenders of Corneille escalated, including an attack by the playwright Claveret and a claim by a Norman noble that Corneille, although ennobled, had refused to fight a duel.[7] In May or June Scudéry appealed to the Academy to settle the issue. Corneille, learning that Richelieu was in favor of a ruling by the Academy, agreed reluctantly. The role of Richelieu in the Quarrel has been a repeated source of scholarly speculation. Tallemant des Réaux, Boileau, Fontenelle, and other critics have argued that Richelieu resented Corneille and *Le Cid:* for Corneille's desertion from the "Five Authors," for the glorification of Spain (with whom France was at war) in the play, for the play's implicit defense of dueling. But it is much more likely that Richelieu's motive was simply to establish the authority and prestige of his newly created (1635) Academy by having it define and clarify the rules of dramatic poetry.[8] After all, Richelieu had the play put on twice at his own palace, allowed Corneille to dedicate it to his niece, and ennobled his family on account of its success; these facts hardly suggest a personal rancor.

Meanwhile, as the *doctes* of the Academy met to consider the issue, the polemic continued. The pamphlets became more heated, their tone more venomous. Finally in October Richelieu intervened to put an end to the unseemly quarrel—by informing Mairet through an intermediary that he wanted a cessation. And so the literary world waited for the Academy's ruling, which finally arrived in December: *Les Sentiments de l'Académie sur Le Cid.*

The *Sentiments* submitted by the Academy had been seen and approved by Richelieu but were largely the work of Jean Chapelain, whose scholarly reputation was such that Richelieu had assigned him the Academy's charge on this issue. In presenting the official view of the Academy, Chapelain produced forty-odd pages of fine print—a document of legalistic criticism, minutely examining Scudéry's charges and some other points as well. The *Sentiments* defended Corneille against some of Scudéry's attacks—and made the observations that, despite the play's faults, the power of its passions and the elevated subtlety of some of its sentiments give the play an inexplicable agreeableness and beauty which charm the spectator.[9]

These points of praise could not have done much to please Corneille, for the list of faults and violations is considerably longer, going further even than Scudéry in its insistence on a strict application of "Aristotelian" rules. Its conclusions, while less severe, were not unlike Scudéry's—that the subject, while charming, was defective; that the resolution was faulty; that the play had too many unnecessary episodes; that some passages were stylistically defective or impure; that verisimilitude, decorum, and propriety were not always observed.

Like Scudéry, Chapelain believed in the utilitarian aim of art; thus, his judgment, too, rested on the relation between *vraisemblance, bienséance,* and morality—the argument that in violating verisimilitude and decorum, the play violated propriety and moral ethics. Supporting Scudéry's major criticisms, Chapelain also felt that Chimène illustrated the triumph of love over duty: *"Nous la blasmons seulement de ce que son amour l'emporte sur son devoir"* ("We blame her only in that her love triumphs over her duty").[10] The criticism is based largely on the distinction between *le vrai* (the real) and *le vraisemblable* (the realistic, verisimilar): art should avoid the unlikely or extraordinary, even if real (it doesn't matter that historically Chimène actually did marry Rodrigue), in favor of more universal and moral truths. As Scudéry had argued in reference to Chimène's marrying her father's murderer: *"Cet événement était bon pour l'historien, mais il ne valait rien pour le poète. . . . Chimène est une parricide"*[11] ("This event is fine for the historian, but it is worth nothing to the poet. . . . Chimène is a parricide"). Other characters were also condemned with the same reasoning: the King acts without appropriate dignity and decorum in tricking Chimène into admitting her love—even more, he offends our moral sense by condoning the marriage; Rodrigue acts unchivalrously and with effrontery in forcing his way into Chimène's quarters after killing her father; and so on. The principle on which such criticism lies is that Corneille sacrificed verisimilitude in favor of the real, with the result that the characters become incredible and morally offensive. Chimène, the Academy argued, was *"une amante trop sensible et fille trop dénaturée"*[12] ("too susceptible a lover and too unnatural a daughter").

In fact, then, the major criticism by both Scudéry and the Academy had less to do with form or with the unities (a popular misconception) than it did with the ethics of verisimilitude. To us today the play's ethical strictures may seem like a moral straitjacket; Corneille's contemporaries, however, complained that it wasn't morally rigorous enough. The essential point of contestation was Chimène's conduct in marrying her father's murderer. Corneille would later argue that the historic sources attest the *truth*, and truth is enough. Like Scudéry, Chapelain argued that the rea*listic* was better than the real (*"Nous maintenons que toutes les vérités ne sont pas bonnes pour le théâtre. . . ."*: "We maintain that not all truths are good for the theatre"),[13] and the real should be modified so as to seem both likely and ethical; Chapelain thus contrived a choice of three "suitable" (and equally absurd) endings preferable to Corneille's. But the debate posed the problem of the real versus the realistic, a central issue in the dogma of classicism: the real or the ideal, and its corollary choice, the pathological or the normal (one might even say the romantic or the classical)? The basic question, finally, is the purpose of art: is art meant to have a moral and dogmatic utility, or is it justified for its own sake? This would be a major source of critical debate for the whole century. While Corneille would later argue that all truth is acceptable in poetry and that art's major function is to please (rather than instruct), the Academy's view that *Le Cid* was unrealistic and unethical gave official and authoritative preference to the direction writers should follow: it was a triumph of classicism over the baroque and romanesque, of "regular" tragedies over tragicomedies and comedies, of the *Anciens* over the *Modernes* (this debate would be prominent for the whole century), of the scholarly tastes of the *doctes* and *savants* over the public tastes of the *ignorants*, of the ethically instructive over the melodramatically entertaining. As Boileau was to argue a few years later, one must *"sauver la bienséance"* ("preserve propriety") because tragedy *"doit enseigner des choses qui main-tiennent la société civile"* ("ought to teach those things which maintain a civilized society"). Thus, the results of the Quarrel—the first open discussion on the aesthetic validity of the "rules"—shaped and gave official approval to what would be the aesthetic tastes and values of the classical age.

Chapelain's long list of violations of *vraisemblance, bienséance,* and ethics was even more casuistically absurd and lacking in dramatic sense (and suspension of disbelief) than was Scudéry's. Lancaster summarizes them thus:

The King should never have proposed that Chimène marry the victor in the judicial contest, nor should she have consented to marry Rodrigue. The fact that her historical prototype married Rodrigue is no excuse. It would have been better for the Count to turn out not to be her father or not to have been killed.[!] As it is, the marriage is inexcusable, unless it can be shown that the safety of the kingdom depended on it. In short, it would have been better not to write the play than to set girls such a deplorable example. Moreover, too many actions are crowded into twenty-four hours, and the characters do not conduct themselves as they should. Rodrigue could have spared the Count in consideration of his love, and should have stabbed himself rather than have asked Chimène to kill him. The heroine ought not to have admitted that Rodrigue was justified in challenging her father and that she hoped her efforts to avenge the latter would be unavailing. She should have been accompanied by her friends to and from the palace, should have, of her own accord, told the king about her love, and should not have refused to marry Sanche when she thought he had won her in the fight with Rodrigue. Don Diègue should not have been allowed by his 500 friends to seek his son alone. The Count should not have begun the play by communicating his views to a *suivante* [follower, servant]. The Infanta is quite useless. The king should have sent guards to prevent the fight between the Count and Rodrigue. Corneille should have explained how Rodrigue got access to Chimène's house. Insufficient time is allowed for the judicial combat, which should not have been followed by Don Sanche's bringing the sword, or by his finding himself unable to explain to Chimène the result of the duel. Finally, it is unfortunate that several places are represented, though this is an objection that can be made to most plays of the time.[14]

In fact, *Le Cid* was much more regular than most plays of the time. But Chapelain's suggestions would rob the play of any dramatic interest or even resemblance to Corneille's conception of it. Founded on *bienséance* and plausibility, Chapelain's views would have the denouement revealing the Count to be either still alive or not in reality Chimène's father! Thus, the very search for verisimilitude would have produced, ironically, an even more implausible and artificial conclusion. As Lancaster says: "Chapelain's criticism is primarily that of a moralist who is blind both to the art of portraying character and to methods of entertaining an audience. Seldom has the academic mind shown itself more obtuse. . . . He dared assert that it would have been better that this play should not have been written than that it should have set an example of lack of respect for a father's memory, however guilty that father might be. The heroic effort of the lovers to do their duty as they understood it meant nothing to him and their love left him cold. He would have preferred a silly plot in which the wounded father came to life at the last moment, and characters that always acted in accordance with a fixed code of behavior. His judgment is, above all, that of the philistine who is offended by an artist's efforts to escape from his toils."[15] Chapelain's assumptions in this kind of dogmatic and legalistic criticism are that a poet writes for critics (rather than for an audience) and that critical judgments can be made according to a set of impartial rules rather than according to personal tastes. As with Edgar Allan Poe's "The Philosophy of Composition," the underlying principle is that you need only apply the right rules and criteria and you will produce a good poem. How well does this philosophy work? In 1656 Chapelain, urged by friends, published an epic poem of his own called *La Pucelle;* it proved unreadable.[16]

Corneille's public reaction to the Académie's official judgment was silence. But privately he was troubled and obsessed by the issues, making numerous revisions to the play. No new work arrived for three years. But then in 1640–42 came *Horace, Cinna,* and *Polyeucte*—three Roman tragedies, incontestably regular and successful masterworks which solidified the classical tragedy as the preferred genre of the age. However, in proving his ability to write dramatically successful plays which nevertheless conformed to the learned classical taste, Corneille had not forgotten the issues of the Quarrel. In his *Avertissement* prefacing the 1648 edition of the collected works and in the *Examens* and the three *Discours* published in the 1660 edition, he would, years after the Quarrel, set down his views and justify himself on these issues. He pointed out that the dramatic rules had been defined, not by practicing playwrights, but by critics and scholars who knew nothing about dramatic staging and presentation; reading Aristotle was not enough to create dramatic genius. In the 1648 *Avertissement* he argued that while *Le Cid* was basically in compliance with Aristotelian rules, he himself was not as much concerned with quibbles over *"des bienséances et des agréments"* ("proprieties and unities") as over the dramatic means of stimulating the audience emotions appropriate to a tragedy.[17] Rejecting the dogmatic utility of art, he claimed that the aim of art is only to please and that the usefulness of the rules is as dramatic means toward producing such pleasure.[18] As for the didactic and moralistic function of literature, he pointed out that "if evil, vice, or weakness were removed from the stage there would be little left of ancient as well as modern theatre."[19] As for *vraisemblance*, the poet must be allowed to have some dramatic flexibility, for the theatre is not reality but illusion. Using Aristotle for support, he pointed out that the emotions involving romantic love and blood ties are the most suitable sources for tragedy—and that tragic events along such lines (such as parricides, and so on) are by their very essence unrealistic, contrary to nature: *"Les grands sujets qui remuent fortement les passions, et en opposent l'impétuosité aux lois du devoir ou aux tendresses du sang, doivent toujours aller au-delà du vraimsemblable"*[20] ("The great subjects which move passions violently, and which set up conflicts with laws of duty or with affections of blood, must always go beyond the realistic"). In his own plays Corneille's most important consideration, he claimed, was the *dramatic* function and value of the work, not its ethics or utilitarian principles.

Nevertheless, the Quarrel was important in being the first open discussion about the rules so central to the period, and in confirming the course of the period as an age to be colored by the classical rather than the baroque. The Academy's support of the rules would later touch off the century-long debate between the Ancients and Moderns, or Regulars and Irregulars. The documents involved in the Quarrel reveal much about Corneille, Mairet, Scudéry, Chapelain, and the critical sentiments of the age; they also forced Corneille to consider the means and purpose of his art—and directed him toward the three Roman classical tragedies which were to follow. And the very nature and purpose of art itself was now an open issue which all major French critics would discuss in the future, beginning with contemporaries like d'Aubignac and Boileau. It was, in the end, much more than a quarrel over *Le Cid* or over Corneille's vaingloriousness.

Other Critical Controversies

The critical debates involving *Le Cid* did not end with the Quarrel, and three subsequent smaller ones are worth mentioning; all, of course, are related to the issues of the Quarrel.

The first is the actual genre appellation of *Le Cid:* what is the appropriate classification for this heroic tale of young love? Most critics (including Adam, Couton, Lancaster, Moore, and Nurse, among others) accept the label of "tragicomedy" given the play at its debut in 1637. But in the 1648 edition Corneille himself changed the subtitle to "tragedy"; while André Stegmann is one who would stand by this later appellation, other critics deny that Corneille's work is tragic at all; Nelson goes so far as to argue that "Neither tragicomedy nor tragedy, *Le Cid* is a romance."[21]

Certainly the audience must have sensed, in watching *Le Cid*, that this was not real life but the realm of shared daydream and fantasy; in that sense, as Moore puts it, "It [the play] is perhaps the perfection of tragicomedy."[22] Corneille may have changed the generic description because by 1648 tragedy had clearly established itself as the more respected and valued of the two genres. But we have also seen how he imbued this tragicomedy with a tragic tone and grandeur, and that he made it a much more regular play than was usual in 1637; by such standards, it could then have been called either a tragicomedy or a tragedy. As P. J. Yarrow points out: "Corneille does not make a clear-cut distinction between comedy and tragedy: his conception of tragedy embraces comedy as well. His characters, given to teasing and irony, fond of using familiar language . . . are human and natural."[23] And as Moore reminds us, the theory about the distinction between genres grew up only in the wake of Racine, and should not be applied to the earlier Corneille.[24] Corneille himself seemed to have viewed his plays largely as dramatic entertainments, often mixing genres, rather than as works in distinct categories.

Strictly speaking, the play is, as Lancaster notes, a tragicomedy: "The struggle contains a tragic element in that the lovers find themselves both oppressed and inspired by the code, which plays the role of ancient Fate, but, as the play was called a tragi-comedy, the author, when enough sacrifice had been made to Honor, allowed Love to triumph."[25] The play in fact had something to please both Classicists and Romanticists. In obeying the twenty-four hour unity of time and the unity of place (in that all action occurs in Seville), in concentrating on a moral issue as its central conflict, and in banishing the battle and the duels offstage, the play had the essential virtues of a classical tragedy. But it is also a perfect example of the elements of tragicomedy: a romanesque theme involving love and war, inspired by a Spanish (rather than classical) source; its basic situation (hero kills lover's father) a dear one to the romantic tradition; its use of secondary plots (the Infante, Don Sanche, the Moors); the happy ending—as well as many specific dramatic and crowd-pleasing touches (the slap, the bloodied sword, the comic moments, the presence of Rodrigue in Chimène's house, and so on): all prove this story to be in the spirit of tragicomedy. As Adam argues, *Le Cid* is not a tragedy but a tragicomedy that adheres to the essences of this romanesque genre; but, as he also points out, Corneille gives the play *"une valeur morale et humaine qu'aucune autre tragi-comédie ne possédait"* ("a moral and human quality which no other tragicomedy possessed").[26] Couton concurs: "In evoking grave issues, [Corneille] conferred on the tragicomedy an authority which the tragic genre itself might envy. But he preserved from tragicomedy the dash, the scenic movement of a cloak-and-dagger drama, a gushing lyricism, the finely good-natured smile of the king" (my translation). As Couton concludes about *Le Cid*'s place in the French canon: "It endures as our one tragicomedy."[27]

A very closely related controversy is the question of whether or not the ending is in fact "happy." In the 1660 *Examen* Corneille suggested that the issue was left unresolved, that Chimène's silence to the King is not a sign of consent but of contradiction, and that we should not necessarily assume a happy ending. Of course Corneille's "clarification" left the ending ambiguous—as he no doubt meant to, after so many accusations of immorality for allowing a girl to marry her father's killer. But there is no such ambiguity in the actual text itself, which clearly has the tone of a tragicomic solution. In our century, only a few critics (notably Nadal and Abraham) have tried to maintain that there is not a happy resolution and eventual wedding implied.[28] There is every indication in the final scene of the forthcoming nuptials, and the only reason they are postponed, as the King explains, is not to leave them in doubt but in deference to Chimène's honor and her shock at the alacrity of the event—when, as it were, the funeral baked meats could still furnish forth the marriage table. In the original version of lines 1806–11 (before Corneille's revisions), Chimène complained that a wedding on the same day *("Qu'un même jour")* as her father's death would "soil my honor with an eternal reproach" *("Et souiller mon honneur d'un reproche éternel").*[29] So the King chooses to let her grow accustomed to the idea and not be forced to marry her father's killer on the same day as her father's death (the latter would not have been a problem had Corneille not tried to obey the twenty-four hour unity of time in the first place):

> What seems at first inexorable crime
> Has oft been made legitimate through time:
> Rodrigue has won you; you are his, it's true,
> But though today his valor conquered you,
> I would needs be your honor's enemy
> To give him the prize of his victory
> So soon. These delayed nuptials don't vacate
> A law which gives you to him, since no date
> Was set. You'll have a year to mourn if you
> Would like.
>
> (1813–22)

Both Rodrigue's last line—"I now can hope, and I am happy, Sir" (1836)—and the King's—"Leave that to time, your valor, and your king" (1840)—leave no doubt as to the expectations of the appropriate and happy event.

A more debatable issue is the presence and role of the Infante. Scudéry first accused the Infante of being a useless subplot and thus of violating the unity of action, and the Academy concurred; Scudéry may well have been correct that Corneille needed to find a major role for La Beauchasteau. Most critics subsequently agreed that the Infante was a superfluous role, and in the eighteenth century the play was almost always played without her, on the classical principle that anything not indispensable is of no value. However, by now we have grown to realize that the Infante does serve some important functions, and she usually is now played in performance. The role serves several functions, both major and minor. On the minor side, there is the dramatic function of added suspense and dramatic interest; as Nelson asks (from the spectator's viewpoint): "What of l'Infante's inclination toward Rodrigue? Will she cast aside her scruples about his inferior station and even possibly use her own station to usurp Chimène's prior claim? . . . And will l'Infante attempt to profit by [the lovers'] separation?"[30] Further, as Bénichou points out, contemporary audiences were especially fond of female "duels," competitions between two women for the love of the same man.[31] Even more useful is the fact that, as was first pointed out in one of the anonymous tracts during the Quarrel, the princess's love for Rodrigue elevates Rodrigue to a royal (and tragic) stature from the very beginning—a stature raised higher still by his victories and his title of Cid; thus, he becomes a hero of exceptional grandeur (*Ça grandit Rodrigue*, Napoleon—who was in the same position—later concurred), which makes more explicable and acceptable Chimène's silence in ceding to him and to the King's wishes at the end. This is no longer a minor function.

So is the Infante really such an irrelevant subplot? She existed in de Castro's Spanish version; and, while Corneille excised all of de Castro's other subplots, he actually increased her role by giving her a tragic grandeur (that is not in the Spanish source) in her internal struggle between her pride of place and her love for Rodrigue. Why? Jean Boorsch has pointed out that "if one looks more closely, one perceives that she is always in a scene adjacent to one in which Chimène appears: it is exactly as if she picked up again, in miniature, and on an alternate theme, the motifs of emotion which Chimène has just developed" (my translation).[32] Or, as Nelson argues even further: "the role constitutes a dramatic as well as a lyrical echo of the main plot. It is a sort of play-within-a-play functioning as a 'mirror,' like the Shakespearean subplot."[33] Similarly, Couton suggests that the Infante gives to the drama of the two lovers *"un subtil contrepoint"* ("a subtle counterpoint").[34] For she poses the conflict of love versus honor from the very beginning of this play—and, in choosing honor over love, shows herself to be a strong woman with admirable *gloire*. I would argue that she serves as foil to *both* Chimene and Rodrigue—since all three face the internal conflict of love and honor; her status within the play in this capacity is suggested by the fact that she is the only other character besides Rodrigue who is given a monologue in *stances*, at the very point (5.2) when she is making her decision to follow honor, as Rodrigue had done in his own *stances* (1.6).

Being a foil to one or both protagonists gives the Infante a major function in terms of unity of action. But how one interprets her role as a foil is also debatable. Some critics have argued that she is stronger than Chimène: she finally doesn't flinch from her duty, bringing Chimène and Rodrigue together so as to extinguish her own love and preserve her honor; thus, the Infante and Chimène would seem to present two versions of "woman," strong and weak, respectively (with Chimène's final admissions of and capitulations to love). But I would agree with Nelson's argument that her presence is in fact not a reproach to Chimène.[35] Rather, it seems to me that while the Infante continually wavers about whether to pursue love or honor, Chimène never does: as soon as her father is killed, Chimène clamors for vengeance, pursuing her *gloire* throughout the play (while still loving Rodrigue)—until, at the end, she is left no recourse but to give in; she never *chooses* love over honor, but always the other way around. And when the Infante does finally renounce her love and opts to give Rodrigue away to Chimène, it seems (under retrospective scrutiny) a sympathetic but empty gesture: he was never hers to give away to begin with, and she knew from the start that he did not love her, that her love was not only contrary to her *gloire* but simply hopeless. Her renunciation of love for honor allows her to maintain her tragic dignity and self-respect, but as a foil her choice suggests to us, by contrast, how much greater is the difficulty (and thus the glory, too) involved in the parallel choices Rodrigue and Chimène make: to be able still to choose honor over a love they know to be both fervent and reciprocal.

Summary of Critical History

Finally, this chapter ends with a *very* brief abstract of historical trends in criticism concerning *Le Cid;* readers interested in a more detailed critical history of Corneille's works are referred to Herbert Fogel's useful volume, *The Criticism of Cornelian Tragedy.*[36] As we have seen, in the seventeenth century criticism of *Le Cid* was primarily centered on the classical principles of verisimilitude, good taste, and decorum; Scudéry, Chapelain, l'Abbé d'Aubignac, Guez de Balzac, Boileau, Saint-Evremond, Madame de Sévigné, and La Bruyère were the major commentators. For them the subject of the play was the conflict between duty and love, and the major objection was that love was allowed to triumph and that the play was thus immoral. They recognized the play's ability to move audiences and its sublimity of sentiment, but felt that its violations of plausibility and propriety left it a morally questionable text.

By the eighteenth century, Cornelian grandeur and the heroic ideal were out of place in an era more concerned with love and less with the heroic; only Voltaire and La Harpe produced major studies of Corneille. They both found an admiration for Cornelian heroes, in whom duty and honor triumphed over love, to seem cold and sterile, and were very critical of the works; ironically, for that same reason they both praised *Le Cid* because it was, as Voltaire argued, the only one of Corneille's plays depicting *"ce combat des passions qui déchire le coeur"* ("this conflict of passions which rends the heart"). They defended the play's plausibility, propriety, and morality—and praised it (in ironic contrast to seventeenth-century critics) for the very fact that it *did* illustrate the triumph of love over duty, since Romantic love was their most treasured ideal: Voltaire wrote that *"Aimer le meurtrier de son père, et poursuivre la vengeance de ce meurtre, était une chose admirable"* ("To love the murderer of her father, and to seek vengeance for this murder, was an admirable thing").[37] Ever since Voltaire's and La Harpe's defense of *Le Cid*, the play has no longer been judged by the rules of verisimilitude and decorum.

In the nineteenth century, supporters of the popular taste for the new Romantic drama (such as Hugo, Stendhal, and Lamartine) were even more hostile to Cornelian tragedy: it was at this time that the notion was born of Cornelian tragedy as a conflict between duty and passion capped by the triumph of stern will and cold determination. The critics felt that drama should portray not only the ideal beauty of the mind but also the passions and even ugliness of reality. For those reasons, *Le Cid* was the most admired of Corneille's plays: Nisard felt that the conflict between love and duty *did* depict reality (*"La lutte de la passion et du devoir, qu'est-ce autre chose en effet que la vie elle-même?"* "The fight between passions and duty, what is it in effect if not life itself?"); and Sainte-Beuve praised the play because it allowed love to triumph: "A young man who did not admire *Le Cid* would be very unfortunate; he would be lacking the passion and the vocation of his age. *Le Cid* is an immortal flower of love and honor" (my translation).[38]

In the late nineteenth century, Brunetière, Faguet, Lemaître, Rigal, and Lanson were the principal Cornelian commentators: to them, Cornelian tragedy seemed even more a cold and stern moralistic conflict between passion and duty, in which the more austere virtue triumphs, a victory of sheer will over the emotions. The opinion of the century was summarized by Brunetière: *"C'est beau, admirable, sublime, ce n'est ni humain, ni vivant, ni réel"*[39] ("It's beautiful, admirable, sublime; its neither human, nor alive, nor real"). By 1898, Lanson was dismissing emotions as playing any significant role in Cornelian theatre: "Tension, the power of the will, this is the whole perspective from which Corneille looks at the human soul."[40] Far removed from the early-seventeenth century ideal of honor and *gloire* as the greatest and warmest of passions, the nineteenth-century critics could only feel that Corneille's tragedies were marked by an absence of passion. In *Le Cid*, they argued, the conflict between love and duty within Rodrigue and Chimène did not entail a real decision, and the interest in the play was largely to observe their determination in executing their duty. However, Lemaître and Faguet noted that in the end it is love that triumphs over duty; and so, ironically, *Le Cid* was again considered (and admired as) an accidental exception among Corneille's works. It is a double irony, because in fact—as we have seen—honor triumphs over love, after a poignant struggle, within both protagonists; but circumstances such as the Moorish battle, the King's decisions, and Chimène's misinterpretation of the results of the duel—allow for love finally to triumph nonetheless, externally. Fogel's comment is appropriate: "The idea that all Cornelian tragedy pits duty against passion and that duty triumphs is erroneous. Most critics agree that *le Cid* portrays a conflict between duty and love, but they maintain that love triumphs. It is singular that Corneille's most celebrated play is perhaps the least typical example of Cornelian tragedy."[41]

In our own century, Cornelian critics have moved from an emphasis on the four major works *(Le Cid, Horace, Cinna,* and *Polyeucte)* to a consideration as well of the comedies and later tragedies; thus, there has been by comparison less specific attention paid to *Le Cid*. Only Schlumberger has felt the need to defend the play's morality, by far the greatest issue in the seventeenth and eighteenth centuries; Brasillach and Adam, while acknowledging the play's romanesque elements, concur with the nineteenth-century critics that the play is a drama of will. But the critics have tended to agree that since the twists in the plot conspire to allow love to triumph over duty, *Le Cid* can be considered a youthful accident/exception in the Cornelian canon. As is the nature of twentieth-century criticism, however, most Cornelian commentary has moved from an organic consideration of a play *in toto* to a study of a specific discipline, genre, or approach: themes (Nadal on love, Nelson on heroes, Herland on the tragic, Bénichou on the heroic); biographical influences (Rivaille, Couton); psychology (Nadal, Schlumberger, Boorsch); period—historical, social, political, ethical—influences (Brasillach, Bénichou, Couton); techniques (May, Boorsch, Schérer); language and metaphor (Crétin, Merian-Genast); genre (Lancaster, Moore, Adam, Schérer); comparative—especially with Racine—studies (Turnell, May, Nurse); and a number of textual studies and critical editions. It is in such focused studies of particular facets of Cornelian drama that the majority of twentieth-century criticism of *Le Cid* is to be found.[42]

Notes

Introduction

1. The study of translation is an excellent way, after all, of investigating "the differences which generally exist between what one literary language will allow and what another will not. This is the most challenging prospect for the future of comparative literature. . . ." G. Watson, *The Study of Literature* (London, 1969). This quotation is cited by André Lefevere, in *Translating Poetry: Seven Strategies and a Blueprint* (Amsterdam: Van Gorcum, 1975), p. 99.

2. Some of the more notable studies on poetic translation include: Dudley Fitts, *The Poetic Nuance* (New York: Harcourt, Brace, 1958); *On Translation*, ed. Reuben A. Brower (Cambridge: Harvard Studies in Comparative Literature, Harvard University Press, 1959); Paul Selver, *The Art of Translating Poetry* (Boston: The Writer, 1966); Vladimir Nabokov, *Notes on Prosody—from the commentary to his translation of Pushkin's "Eugene Onegin"* (New York: Pantheon Books, 1964); Allen Tate, *The Translation of Poetry* (Washington, D.C.: U.S. Govt. Printing Office, 1972); C. Day Lewis, *On Translating Poetry* (Abingdon-on-Thames, 1970); George Steiner, *After Babel: Aspects of Language and Translation* (Oxford: Oxford University Press, 1975); André Lefevere, *Translating Poetry: Seven Strategies and a Blueprint* (Assen/Amsterdam: Van Gorcum, 1975); Ben Belitt, *Adam's Dream: A Preface to Translation* (New York: Grove Press, 1978); John Felstiner, *Translating Neruda: The Way to Machu Picchu* (Stanford: Stanford University Press, 1981).

3. The eight modern verse translations I have come across are: Florence Kendrick Cooper, in *Great Plays—French and German* (New York: D. Appleton & Co., 1904); Paul Landis, *Six Plays by Corneille and Racine* (New York: Modern Library, 1931); John C. Lapp, *Le Cid* (Arlington Heights, Ill.: AHM Publishing Corp., 1955); Lacy Lockert, *The Chief Plays of Corneille* (Princeton: Princeton University Press, 1957); James Schevill, *Le Cid*, in *The Classic Theatre*, vol. 4, ed. Eric Bentley (Garden City, N.Y.: Doubleday, 1961); Kenneth Muir, *The Cid*, in *Seventeenth-Century French Drama*, ed. Jacques Guicharnaud (New York: Modern Library, 1967); Samuel Solomon, *Pierre Corneille: Seven Plays* (New York: Random House, 1969); John Cairncross, *Pierre Corneille* (Baltimore: Penguin Books, 1975). Of these, the sole couplet translation is Mr. Schevill's; the rest are predominantly blank verse. However, I should note that Mr. Solomon's translation is a curious hybrid, neither flesh nor fowl—largely in blank verse but shifting into rhyme at moments of intensity; Shakespeare may be an arguable precedent for this practice in English drama, but the effect, in my view, is very awkward in the more homogeneous French tradition.

4. André Lefevere, *Translating Poetry*, pp. 98, 49.

5. "Faithfulness," as I have defined it, requires that the translation not only provide a

semantic equivalence in the translator's language, but that this equivalence be fashioned in such a way as to reflect the powerful influence on it of the original tongue and of its socioliterary conventions. My own translation has tried to adhere to this principle.

6. As the French linguist Antoine Meillet puts it, *"tout vocabulaire exprime une civilisation"* ("every vocabulary expresses a civilization"). Meillet, *Linguistique historique et linguistique générale*, vol. 2 (Paris: Klincksieck, 1938), p. 145.

7. Strictly speaking, 1,840 lines in *Le Cid*. The text of the play I have used throughout this endeavor is the fine *Nouveaux Classiques Larousse* edition of *Le Cid* (Paris: Librairie Larousse, 1959).

8. Obviously all other eight verse translators of *Le Cid* have likewise concluded iambic pentameter to be the best solution: seven wrote in blank verse, one in iambic pentameter couplets. Similarly, in 1957 Lacy Lockert wrote, in his "Translator's Foreword," that "all English metrical translations of Corneille made within the last hundred years have been, to the best of my knowledge, in blank verse." *Chief Plays*, p. xii.

9. One should not be allowed to criticize without taking the same risk; thus, my version:

> My father's dead. I saw him when he died,
> His blood, Sir, streaming from his noble side.

10. Mr. Schevill sometimes even loses count of his iambs, as in this line (785:3.2): "Its course is often lost in time."

11. In his analysis of various methodologies of poetic translation (based on comparing translations of Catullus #64), Professor Lefevere sees the rhymer's dilemma as hopelessly unredeemable: "The rhyming translator enters into a double bondage. He is confronted with problems of both metre and rhyme. He does not tie himself to the metre of the source text, as the purely metrical translator usually does, but he soon finds out that the restrictions of a self-imposed metre are just as severe. Unlike his metrical colleague he must always be on the look-out for the rhyme word, and he is therefore even more restricted in his freedom of choice. The demands of metre, the demands of rhyme, and the demands of metre and rhyme combined have to be met. The problem is difficult enough to solve in the case of an original poem. In the case of a translation, in which rhyme and metre have to be modelled to match pre-selected and pre-arranged materials, the search for a satisfactory solution is doomed to failure from the start." *Translating Poetry*, 49.

12. My version:

> INFANTE: I love—
> LEONOR: You love him!
> INFANTE: *(taking Leonor's hand)*   Feel my heart beat faster
>   And flutter at the mention of its master;
>   It knows him.
> LEONOR: Forgive me, Madame, if I . . .

I take advantage of a stage direction to aid me here.

13. An example from Mr. Schevill (857–58:3.4):

> RODRIGO: Then speak to me with my despairing sword.
> CHIMENA: My father's blood like some dumb beast you've gored!

14. John Cairncross, translating *Le Cid*, writes: "I rapidly discovered that nothing was easier than to produce a version which would strike our irreverent age as an uproariously comic caricature. It was essential, therefore, to elaborate a style which would render, at least to some extent, the sustained 'nobility' of Corneille's world." *Pierre Corneille*, p. 9.

15. In fairness to Lowell, we should note that he calls his translation of *Phèdre* a "version"—

and, as such, it is an interesting, vigorous, and admirable experiment. But it is not "faithful" to the original tongue and its socio-literal conventions (see note 5). *Phaedra*, English Version by Robert Lowell, in *The Classic Theatre*, vol. 4, ed. Eric Bentley (Garden City, N.Y.: Doubleday, 1961). The quoted French text is taken from Jean Racine, *Phèdre* (Paris: Librairie Larousse, 1959), p. 35.

16. Paul Bénichou, *Morales du Grand Siècle* (Paris: Editions Gallimard, 1948).

17. To us today, a play like *Le Cid* seems both a moral as well as technical straitjacket. To Corneille's contemporaries it was, in fact, not controlled and disciplined enough. Richelieu himself brought it before the French *Académie*, as part of a celebrated literary controversy which condemned the play for being scandalously immoral and much too careless with the unities. (See also Chapter 5).

18. Landis, *Six Plays*, p. xii.

19. Lockert, *Chief Plays*, p. xi.

20. The other blank verse versions: Cairncross: "O miracle of love! O crowning woe! / How many ills our fathers dead will cause! / Who would have thought so? Who'd have said so? Ah! / Our happiness so near was lost so soon"; Cooper: "O miracle of love! O weight of woe! / We pay our filial debt in suffering! / Roderick, who would have thought—Or could have dreamed—/ That joy so near so soon our grasp would miss?"; Landis: "O miracle of love! O weight of woe! / What sufferings and tears our fathers cost us! / Roderick, who had thought— Who would have dreamed—/ That joy so near us should so soon be lost?"; Lapp: "O wondrous love! / O heavy pain! What tears our fathers cost us! / Who could believe, Rodrigue? Or who foretell? / Our happiness, so near, should swiftly vanish?"; Muir: "Miracle of love! O heap of miseries! / How many woes and tears our fathers cost us! / Who would believe . . . Chimene, who would have said . . . / That happiness which seemed within our grasp / Would be destroyed so soon?"

21. My version:

> Yes, I know your love—so don't reply;
> But live in shame and you deserve to die.

22. Ben Belitt writes: "For me, translation remains the sensuous approximation of an amateur . . . and, I would always want to add, my *pleasure*." So also mine. *Adam's Dream*, pages 19–20.

(There are no notes to chapter 1.)

Chapter 2: The Political and Social Milieu

1. André Maurois, *A History of France*, trans. Henry L. Binsse (New York: Minerva, 1968), 193.

2. Ibid., 195.

3. Robert J. Nelson, *Corneille: His Heroes and Their Worlds* (Philadelphia: University of Pennsylvania Press, 1963), 82.

4. Maurois, *A History*, 196.

5. Claude Abraham, *Pierre Corneille* (New York: Twayne, 1972), 22.

6. The quotation is from a discussion of Brasillach's views by Herbert Fogel, in *The Criticism of Cornelian Tragedy* (New York: Exposition Press, 1967), 101.

7. Paul Bénichou, *Man and Ethics: Studies in French Classicism*, trans. Elizabeth Hughes (New York: Doubleday, 1971), 30, 32.

8. Ibid., 2.

9. Ibid., 2.

10. Ibid., 5.

11. As the Nouveaux Classiques Larousse edition of *Le Cid* reminds us, this was the generation of figures such as Montmorency-Bouteville (who defied the edicts of Richelieu), the Cardinal de Retz, the Count of Soissons, the Marquis of Cinq-Mars, the Duke Henri de Guise—dashing *grands seigneurs* much admired for their adventurous exploits full of risk and ambition. *Le Cid* (Paris: Nouveaux Classiques Larousse, 1959), 18.

12. "L'héroisme cornélien correspond à une époque de notre histoire où l'énergie personnelle était au contraire considérée comme la plus haute des valeurs." Antoine Adam, *Le Théâtre Classique* (Paris: Presses Universitaires de France, 1970), 58.

13. Martin Turnell, *The Classical Moment: Studies of Corneille, Molière, and Racine* (London: Hamish Hamilton, 1947), 2.

14. Daniel Mornet, *Histoire de la littérature et de la pensée françaises* (Paris, 1927), 75; quoted in Turnell, *Classical Moment*, 7.

15. Turnell, *Classical Moment*, 11.

16. Turnell's comparison is interesting: "This is the basic difference between the English and French writers of the seventeenth century. It was not for themselves or their society that the English writers feared; they were the victims of an *angoisse métaphysique* which led them to doubt the ultimate sanity of the universe and which made the French confidence unthinkable for them." Ibid., 12.

17. "Faire un corps et [à] s'assembler sous une autorité publique"; the translation is mine. See George H. Gifford, *La France à travers les siècles* (New York: Macmillan, 1936), 125.

18. Bénichou, *Man and Ethics*, 38.

19. Henry Carrington Lancaster, *A History of French Dramatic Literature in the Seventeenth Century*, Part II (The Period of Corneille, 1635–1651), vol. 1 (Baltimore: Johns Hopkins, 1932), 12–13.

20. Ibid., 125.

21. Georges Couton, *Corneille* (Paris: Hatier, 1958), 47.

22. Bénichou, *Man and Ethics*, 47.

23. As Bénichou notes: "In the voice of Don Gormas, and even in that of Rodrigue and Don Diègue, the audience could recognize, as Sainte-Beuve says, 'the echo of that proud and feudal arrogance that Richelieu barely managed to beat down and to crush.'" *Man and Ethics*, 49, citing Sainte-Beuve, *Nouveaux lundis*, vol. 3, articles on Corneille, 1864.

24. Ibid., 47–48.

25. Claude Abraham, in speculating on Corneille's relationship to Richelieu and on Corneille's decision to quit the "Five Authors" group the Cardinal had founded, suggests that while Richelieu may have referred the Quarrel to the Academy only in order to establish the newly created (1635) institution's authority and while Richelieu continued to patronize Corneille, he resented Corneille's individualistic pride: "Corneille, proud and sure of his talents, refused to bow to the wishes of the cardinal and become a hack in a stable of literary mediocrities. Richelieu, equally proud, undoubtedly tried to lower Corneille's stock and, to some extent, succeeded." *Pierre Corneille*, 18.

26. Bénichou, *Man and Ethics*, 49.

27. Ibid., 49.

28. *Le Cid*, Nouveaux Classiques Larousse edition, 56.

29. Bénichou, *Man and Ethics*, 50.

Chapter 3: The French Theatre at the Time of *Le Cid*

1. Jacques Schérer, *La Dramaturgie classique en France* (Paris: Nizet, 1950), 434; the translation is from Will G. Moore, *The Classical Drama of France* (London: Oxford University Press, 1971), 9.

2. Lytton Strachey commented, in his studies of Racine, that "Englishmen have always

loved Molière. It is hardly an exaggeration to say that they have always detested Racine." The latter comment might also be made of Corneille. See Martin Turnell, *The Classical Moment: Studies of Corneille, Molière, and Racine* (London: Hamish Hamilton, 1947), vii. Strachey, *Landmarks in French Literature* (London, 1912), and *Books and Characters* (London, 1922).

3. *Classical Moment*, 5. While Turnell's comparison here is interesting, his study of the period undervalues Corneille incomprehensibly, dismissing him with what Robert J. Nelson refers to as "Martin Turnell's summary interpretations . . . in *The Classical Moment*." Nelson, 14.

4. Turnell, *Classical Moment*, 10–11.

5. Moore, *Classical Drama*, 1.

6. Georges May, "Introduction" to his edition of *Polyeucte* and *Le Menteur* (New York: Dell, 1963), 24–25.

7. Moore, *Classical Drama*, 3.

8. Antoine Adam, *Le Théâtre classique* (Paris: Presses Universitaires de France, 1970), 44–45.

9. Henry Carrington Lancaster, *A History of French Dramatic Literature in the Seventeenth Century*, Part II, vol. 1 (Baltimore: Johns Hopkins, 1932), 14–15.

10. Bénichou shows, however, how Corneille's concept of a tragic hero derives as much from the feudal-chivalric tradition of heroism as from Greek and Roman models. Paul Bénichou, *Man and Ethics: Studies in French Classicism*, trans. Elizabeth Hughes (Garden City, N.Y.: Anchor-Doubleday, 1971), 1–45.

11. Adam, *Le Théâtre classique*, 41.

12. D'Aubignac, *La Pratique du théâtre*, cited by Herbert Fogel, *The Criticism of Cornelian Tragedy* (New York: Exposition Press, 1967), 22–23; the translation is mine.

13. Fogel, *Criticism*, 16.

14. Fontenelle, "Vie de Corneille l'aîné," in *Le Théâtre de Pierre Corneille* (Paris, 1738), 2:lxxx; also quoted in Rémy G. Saisselin's *The Rule of Reason and the Ruses of the Heart: A Philosophical Dictionary of Classical French Criticism, Critics, and Aesthetic Issues* (Cleveland: Case Western Reserve University Press, 1970), 176.

15. From *Les Visionnaires*, lines 579 ff., quoted in Moore, *Classical Drama*, 44.

16. Lancaster, *History*, 5, 1.

17. Peter H. Nurse, *Classical Voices: Studies of Corneille, Racine, Molière, Mme de Lafayette* (London: George G. Harrap, 1971), 16–17.

18. As Moore writes, there was "the emergence of a taste for, and a skill in supplying, *dramatic* material, that is material that conveys suspense, heightened interest, a problem or a conflict moving towards an end that shall be followed and desired and enjoyed by an audience. . . . [which] would not stand for mere lamentation, or for rhetoric that had no dramatic function . . . [and which] included a critical element, people who were later to insist on regular and stylized drama, on plays of maximum concentration, of single appeal, in a dramatic form that should convey the comic or the tragic but not both at once, in verse that allowed them to glimpse their own dilemmas while they watched those of ancient or great persons . . . [and which would] supply what Renaissance experiments lacked, an interest in gesture and word which would hold the attention of a modern audience. It was a basis on which skillful artists might create a classical play." *Classical Drama*, 27.

19. Ibid., 26.

20. Lancaster, *History*, 7.

21. Ibid., 18. G. Vedier makes an interesting argument about the curtain on stage, which he claims was not used to show changes of time and place, but rather to reveal décor, "preventing the décor from being shut off between acts, and making any change of time and place seem improbable. It thus seals the victory of the Rules." Vedier, *Origine et évolution de la dramaturgie néo-classique* (1955), 35; quoted in Moore, *Classical Drama*, 33.

22. See Adam, *Le Théâtre classique*, 23.

23. Moore, *Classical Drama*, 37.

24. Lancaster, *History*, 72.

25. This 1637 English translation of *Le Cid* was made by Joseph Rutter, a poet and friend of Ben Jonson, who had been commissioned to translate it by the Earl of Dorset, lord chamberlain to Queen Henrietta Maria, a princess of France (which may explain how the play arrived at the English court so soon after its Parisian success). The translation is in blank verse, and, according to the title-page, "was acted before their Majesties at Court, and on the Cock-pit Stage in Drury Lane, by the servants to both their Majesties." I am indebted to Mr. S. Y. Huang for pointing out to me the existence of this translation, and to L. le R. Dethan, Curator of The British Library, for information about the translation and for steering me to an extant copy of it.

26. Lancaster, *History*, 118.

27. Moore, *Classical Drama*, 38.

28. Adam, *Le Théâtre classique*, 55–56.

29. Lancaster, *History*, 123.

30. Nurse, *Classical Voices*, 20.

31. Lancaster, *History*, 129.

32. See ibid., 144–51. All three sequels were absurd, especially one described thus in Lancaster: "When the play begins, Chimène has espoused Rodrigue, but is haunted by her father's ghost. Her brother returns from abroad, challenges and kills Rodrigue, becomes a national hero by defeating the Moors, and is rewarded with the Infanta's hand, while Chimène retires from the world. The lesson to be drawn is that it is inadvisable to marry the murderer of one's father." This strikes me as less a sequel to *Le Cid* than a cockeyed version of *Hamlet*.

33. Ibid., 144.

34. See *Le Cid* (Nouveaux Classiques Larousse), 10, and Lancaster, *History*, 144.

35. Lancaster, *History*, 12.

36. Ibid., 6.

Chapter 4: *Le Cid:* The Conflict of Love and Honor

1. Claude Abraham, *Pierre Corneille* (New York: Twayne, 1972), 54.

2. Henry Carrington Lancaster, *A History of French Dramatic Literature in the Seventeenth Century*, Part II, vol. 1 (Baltimore: Johns Hopkins, 1932), 27.

3. Though, as I discuss in chapter 5, the fact (a historical one) that Chimène married Rodrigue at all was still made into an issue in the Quarrel.

4. See Lancaster, *History*, 123, for a full list of these scenes. A more detailed summary of the full action of de Castro's play can be found (in French) in the Nouveaux Classiques Larousse edition of *Le Cid*, pages 13–14.

5. Lancaster, *History*, 123.

6. Herbert Fogel, *The Criticism of Cornelian Tragedy* (New York: Exposition Press, 1967), 9.

7. Paul Bénichou, *Man and Ethics: Studies in French Classicism*, trans. Elizabeth Hughes (Garden City, N.Y.: Anchor-Doubleday, 1971), 2.

8. Ibid., 3.

9. F. Brunetière, *Études critiques sur l'histoire de la littérature française* (Paris: Hachette, 1891); J. Lemaître, *Pierre Corneille*, in L. Petit de Julleville's *Histoire de la langue et de la littérature françaises* (Paris: Armand Colin, 1897); Gustave Lanson, *Corneille* (Paris: Hachette, 1898).

10. Peter H. Nurse, *Classical Voices: Studies of Corneille, Racine, Molière, Mme de Lafayette* (London: George G. Harrap, 1971), 26.

11. Antoine Adam, *Le Théâtre classique* (Paris: Presses Universitaires de France, 1970), 59.

12. Ibid. 60; again my translation.

13. Bénichou, *Man and Ethics*, 5.

14. Ibid., 8.

15. Ibid., 24.

16. Ibid., 28, points out the irony that courtly morality is always "strongly contested by the strict moralists, to whose rank [Corneille] allegedly belongs" (according to critics who misread him as an advocate of moralistic duty and will).

17. Robert J. Nelson, *Corneille: His Heroes and Their Worlds* (Philadelphia: University of Pennsylvania Press, 1963), 69, 71.

18. Ibid., 83.

19. Lancaster, *History*, 124.

20. Abraham, *Pierre Corneille*, 49.

21. Lancaster, *History*, 124.

22. Bénichou, *Man and Ethics*, 34.

23. Abraham, *Pierre Corneille*, 58.

24. Bénichou, *Man and Ethics*, 35, points out that "If the Cid had been Lancelot, he would undoubtedly have forsaken his father and his glory rather than grieve Chimène." Repeatedly Rodrigue vows that there is nothing he would not do or risk for the sake of love.

25. Octave Nadal, *Le Sentiment de l'amour dans l'oeuvre de Pierre Corneille* (Paris: Gallimard, 1948), 164.

26. Bénichou, *Man and Ethics*, 36.

27. Lancaster, *History*, 127.

28. My translation; Nadal, *Le Sentiment de l'amour*, 166.

29. Rodrigue here is a bit like Roland (in the *Chanson de Roland*) at the moment of death, thinking not of love but only of lineage. Bénichou, *Man and Ethics*, 34, in describing the "anti-love tradition" of the old warrior ethic, notes that "The dying Roland thinks of his conquests, of the 'men of his lineage,' of Charles, his lord, and nothing else."

30. Nelson, *Corneille*, 73. Nelson similarly notes that "The language of the famous *stances* is affective rather than analytical. . . . at this moment Rodrigue simply chooses his father over his mistress. The process is dramatic, a conflict between two emotionally charged choices." Ibid., 72–73.

31. Georges Couton, *Corneille* (Paris: Hatier, 1958), 43.

32. "To Lucasta, Going to the Wars."

33. E. Faguet, *En Lisant Corneille* (Paris: Hachette, 1913).

34. Nadal, *Le Sentiment de l'amour*, 168.

35. My translation; ibid., 169.

36. Bénichou, *Man and Ethics*, 43.

37. Nelson, *Corneille*, 75–76.

38. Ibid., 80.

39. Lancaster, *History*, 128.

40. Nadal, *Le Sentiment de l'amour*, 178.

41. See ibid., 169–74.

42. Abraham, *Pierre Corneille*, 57. Abraham goes on to argue that "It is in this context that the role of the Infante is most readily explained: it is particularly when contrasted with the Infante's femininity that Chimène's intransigence is obvious."

43. See Fogel, *Criticism*, 19.

Chapter 5: "The Quarrel of *Le Cid*" and Other Critical Controversies

1. This section is especially indebted to the detailed discussions of this episode in French literary history in Herbert Fogel, *The Criticism of Cornelian Tragedy: A Study of Critical Writing from the Seventeenth to the Twentieth Century* (New York: Exposition Press, 1967); in

Peter H. Nurse, *Classical Voices: Studies of Corneille, Racine, Molière, Mme de Lafayette* (London: George G. Harrap, 1971); and particularly in Henry Carrington Lancaster's monumental *A History of French Dramatic Literature in the Seventeenth Century,* Part II, vol. 1 (Baltimore: Johns Hopkins, 1932).

2. See Lancaster, *History,* 130–31, for full text.

3. Ibid., 132.

4. *Le Cid,* Nouveaux Classiques Larousse, 20.

5. Lancaster, *History,* 132.

6. Ibid., 133. Lancaster attributes these three pamphlets to, possibly, Faret, Sirmond, and Sorel.

7. See ibid., 134, for details.

8. See the Nouveaux Classiques Larousse edition of *Le Cid,* 19, and Lancaster, *History,* 135.

9. So also Guez de Balzac wrote Scudéry that: "*C'est quelque chose de plus d'avoir satisfait tout un Royaume, que d'avoir fait une pièce regulière*" ("It is something greater to have pleased an entire realm than to have written a 'regular' play"). Boileau and La Bruyère similarly admired the play's ability to move audiences through its love element. See Fogel, *Criticism,* 21–22. As Fogel notes: "Scudéry seems to have been the only major critic of the period who did not admit that while *le Cid* failed to observe the essential precepts of the classical doctrine, it nonetheless conveys an impressive sense of beauty."

10. See ibid., 20.

11. See Nurse, *Classical Voices,* 21.

12. See ibid., 21.

13. See ibid., 22.

14. Lancaster, *History,* 140.

15. Ibid., 140.

16. See Remy G. Saisselin, *The Rule of Reason and the Ruses of the Heart: A Philosophical Dictionary of Classical French Criticism, Critics, and Aesthetic Issues* (Cleveland: Case Western Reserve University Press, 1970), 234.

17. See Lancaster, *History,* 141, for the French passage.

18. "*Pour en faciliter les moyens au poète*" ("to facilitate the means for the poet"). This is in the Preface to *Médée;* see Fogel, *Criticism,* 17.

19. From Saisselin, *The Rule of Reason,* 241, citing Corneille's *Discours de l'utilité et des parties du poème dramatique.*

20. From the *Discours du poème dramatique;* see Nurse, *Classical Voices,* 25.

21. Stegmann, *L'Héroisme cornélien* (Paris: Colin, 1968). Robert J. Nelson, *Corneille: His Heroes and Their Worlds* (Philadelphia: University of Pennsylvania Press, 1963), 87. See also Claude Abraham, *Pierre Corneille* (New York: Twayne, 1972), 59.

22. Will G. Moore, *The Classical Drama of France* (London: Oxford University Press, 1971), 38.

23. P. J. Yarrow, *Corneille* (New York: St. Martin's, 1963), 176.

24. See Moore, *Classical Drama,* 39.

25. Lancaster, *History,* 123.

26. Adam, *Le Théâtre classique,* 56.

27. Georges Couton, *Corneille* (Paris: Hatier, 1958), 51, 50.

28. See Octave Nadal, *Le Sentiment de l'amour dans l'oeuvre de Pierre Corneille* (Paris: Gallimard, 1948); and Abraham, *Pierre Corneille,* 59.

29. See the Nouveaux Classiques Larousse edition, 130.

30. Nelson, *Corneille,* 71–72.

31. Paul Bénichou, *Man and Ethics: Studies in French Classicism,* trans. Elizabeth Hughes (Garden City, N.Y.: Anchor-Doubleday, 1971), 11.

32. Boorsch, "Remarques sur la technique dramatique de Corneille," in *Studies by Members*

of the French Department of Yale University, ed. Albert Feuillerat (New Haven: Yale University Press, 1941), 121. Cited by Nelson, *Corneille,* 84.

33. Nelson, *Corneille,* 84.

34. Couton, *Corneille,* 43.

35. Nelson, *Corneille,* 84–86.

36. (New York: Exposition Press, 1967); my brief summary of critical history is much indebted to Fogel's text.

37. See Fogel, *Criticism,* 40.

38. See ibid., 59, for the full Nisard and Sainte-Beuve passages.

39. Cited in Martin Turnell, *The Classical Moment: Studies of Corneille, Molière, and Racine* (London: Hamish Hamilton, 1947), 19.

40. Lanson, *Corneille,* 1898; cited in Bénichou, *Man and Ethics,* 4.

41. Fogel, *Criticism,* 76.

42. See Nelson, *Corneille,* 13–25, for a more detailed summary of modern Cornelian criticism.

Select Bibliography

The following is a very brief and necessarily limited selection of works, in both English and French, for further reading.

Works in English

Abraham, Claude. *Pierre Corneille*. New York: Twayne, 1972.

Bénichou, Paul. *Man and Ethics: Studies in French Classicism*. Trans. Elizabeth Hughes. Garden City, N.Y.: Anchor-Doubleday, 1971. (Translation of Bénichou's *Morales du Grand Siècle*.)

Fogel, Herbert. *The Criticism of Cornelian Tragedy: A Study of Critical Writing from the Seventeenth to the Twentieth Century*. New York: Exposition Press, 1967.

Lancaster, Henry Carrington. *A History of French Dramatic Literature in the Seventeenth Century*. 9 vols. Baltimore: Johns Hopkins Press, 1929–42. Part II ("The Period of Corneille, 1635–1651"), vol. 1, is particularly pertinent.

Lockert, Lacy. *Studies in French Classical Tragedy*. Nashville: Vanderbilt University Press, 1958.

Moore, Will G. *The Classical Drama of France*. London: Oxford University Press, 1971.

Nelson, Robert J. *Corneille: His Heroes and Their Worlds*. Philadelphia: University of Pennsylvania Press, 1963.

Nurse, Peter H. *Classical Voices: Studies of Corneille, Racine, Molière, Mme de Lafayette*. London: George G. Harrap, 1971.

Saisselin, Remy G. *The Rule of Reason and the Ruses of the Heart: A Philosophical Dictionary of Classical French Criticism, Critics, and Aesthetic Issues*. Cleveland: Case Western Reserve University Press, 1970.

Turnell, Martin. *The Classical Moment: Studies of Corneille, Molière, and Racine*. London: Hamish Hamilton, 1947.

Yarrow, P. J. *Corneille.* New York: St. Martin's, 1963.

―――. *A Literary History of France. Volume 2: The Seventeenth Century, 1600–1715.* New York: Barnes and Noble, 1967.

Works In French

Adam, Antoine. *Histoire de la littérature française au dix-septième siècle.* 5 vols. Paris: Domat, 1949–56.

―――. *Le Théâtre classique.* Paris: Presses Universitaires de France, 1970.

Bénichou, Paul. *Morales du grand siècle.* Paris: Gallimard, 1948.

Boorsch, Jean. "Remarques sur la technique dramatique de Corneille." In *Studies by Members of the French Department of Yale University,* ed. Albert Feuillerat. New Haven: Yale University Press, 1941. Pages 101–62.

Brasillach, Robert. *Pierre Corneille.* Paris: Arthème Fayard, 1938.

Corneille, Pierre. *Le Cid.* Paris: Nouveaux Classiques Larousse, 1959.

―――. *Oeuvres.* 2 vols. Paris: La Pléiade, 1950.

Couton, Georges. *Corneille.* Paris: Hatier, 1958.

Doubrowski, Serge. *Corneille et la dialectique du héros.* Paris: Gallimard, 1965.

Faguet, Emile. *En lisant Corneille.* Paris: Hachette, 1913.

Herland, Louis. *Corneille par lui-même.* Paris: Aux Editions du Seuil, 1954.

May, Georges. *Tragédie cornélienne, tragédie racinienne: Etude sur les sources de l'intérêt dramatique.* Urbana: University of Illinois Press, 1948.

Nadal, Octave. *Le Sentiment de l'amour dans l'oeuvre de Pierre Corneille.* Paris: Gallimard, 1948.

Rivaille, Louis. *Les Débuts de Pierre Corneille.* Paris: Boivin, 1936.

Schérer, Jacques. *La Dramaturgie classique en France.* Paris: Nizet, 1950.

Schlumberger, Jean. *Plaisir à Corneille.* Paris: Gallimard, 1936.

Stegmann, André. *L'Héroisme cornélien.* 2 vols. Paris: Colin, 1968.